DATE DUE			
JE 07 '94			
JE 50 '94			
JE 90 '94			
JE 09 '94			
OC 25 '94			
MY 25 '95			
AG 16 '95			

WAYNE
GRETZKY

WAYNE GRETZKY

JOSEPH ROMAIN and JAMES DUPLACEY

Crescent Books

New York

4075693

This 1992 edition published by Crescent Books,
distributed by Outlet Book Company, Inc.,
a Random House Company,
225 Park Avenue South,
New York, New York 10003.

Produced by
Brompton Books Corporation
15 Sherwood Place,
Greenwich, CT 06830

ISBN 0-517-06992-X

8 7 6 5 4 3 2 1

Printed and bound in Hong Kong

This book has not been authorized by and has no connection with Wayne Gretzky.

Page 1: Young phenom Wayne Gretzky.

Page 2: The Los Angeles Kings' Wayne Gretzky in action.

Pages 4-5: Gretzky shoots while airborne in this 1983 Stanley Cup action photo.

Photo Credits
AP/Wide World Photos: 18, 23, 39, 43 bottom.
© Bruce Bennett Studios: 2, 4, 6, 7, 10, 11, 15, 19 both, 20, 21 top, 22 both, 25, 26, 27 both, 28-29, 30, bottom 31 left, 33 both, 35 top, 36 both, 37, 38, 40, 41, 42, 43 top, 44, 45 both, 46, 47 both, 48, 49, 51 both, 52 all, 53, 55, 56-57, 58 both, 59, 60, 61 both, 63 top, 64 both, 69 top 70, 71, 72, 73, 74 both, 75, 76, 78; Bruce Miller: 9.
The Brantford Expositor: 1, 8, 12, 13 both, 14, 16, 17.
Brompton Photo Libarary: 34.
Canadian National Institute for the Blind: 79.
Canapress Photo Service: 68, 69 bottom.
Canapress Photo Service/Doug Ball: 66, 67 bottom; Bruce Edwards: 54; Ray Giguere: 65; John Mahoney: 67 top.
UPI/Bettmann Newsphotos: 21 bottom, 24, 30 top, 31 right, 32, 35 bottom, 50, 62, 63 bottom, 77 both.

CONTENTS

INTRODUCTION: THE GREAT GRETZKY 6
CHAPTER 1 A STAR IS BORN 12
CHAPTER 2 THE EDMONTON YEARS 18
CHAPTER 3 THE DEAL OF THE CENTURY 34
CHAPTER 4 KING GRETZKY 42
CHAPTER 5 GRETZKY'S FIRST AUTOBIOGRAPHY 54
CHAPTER 6 SUMMER HOCKEY: THE INTERNATIONAL STORY ...66
CHAPTER 7 THE GRETZKY EMPIRE 76
INDEX 80

INTRODUCTION:
THE GREAT GRETZKY

Like any sport, hockey is a game with a varied cast of characters. Hockey teams are composed of grinders, policemen, blueline patrolmen, solid goal scorers, netminders, stars and superstars. They all have their roles to play in the winter drama, but none has played his role so well as Number 99, Wayne Gretzky, the consummate superstar.

Since his emergence onto the frozen stage that is ice hockey, Wayne Gretzky has given the sports world plenty to marvel over. At the age of 10, he began a goal-scoring spree that still leaves the hockey world breathless, compiling 378 goals in a single season. For the last 20 years he has continued to silence a singularly critical press with achievement after remarkable achievement. Gretzky has shown consistency by becoming the highest scoring player in the history

Opposite: *Wayne Gretzky – the greatest hockey player to ever play the game.*

Right: *This is a familiar sight, Gretzky passing to a teammate for a shot on goal.*

of the game, has persevered and triumphed under adverse circumstances, and owns the best teamsmanship record in professional sports.

Gretzky is hardly a flash in the hockey pan; year in and year out 'The Great One' has dominated the statistics of the National Hockey League. The secret of Gretzky's play is his ability to envision what will happen before it does. In the bang and clatter of the shifting play, he will always be seen positioning himself for the setup yet to come. However, despite his wide array of scoring marks, Gretzky has revolutionized hockey with his skills as a passer by perfecting the art of delivering the puck to the spot the player will be, not to where he is. Though this sounds simple enough, the consistent application of the principle has placed Wayne Gretzky head and shoulders above the greatest players of our time.

Gretzky has shown a keen ability to amend his playing style to stay ahead of the coaching strategies designed to slow him down, or to keep him out of the action. He is no one-trick pony, however, and sending more men after 'The Kid' has proved to be a costly strategy; covering Gretzky means being drawn out of the fray, leaving his formidable teammates open to fire at will. Gretzky has always been a team player, and though he is clearly frustrated when being

shut down by a dogged pair of shadows, he makes the greatest use of the situation, drawing the heat away and giving the advantage to his mates.

Gretzky works hard to stay ahead, but he was clearly born with a gift. From his precocious beginnings in Brantford, Ontario, where he played with kids much older than himself, through his junior hockey years where his gangly frame was exposed to the rough-and-tumble of the cream of the hopeful Canadian crop, he has stood at the top of the standings and has been the center of attention on and off the ice. From that time to this, he has continued to dominate the game.

Gretzky made his professional debut with the Indianapolis Racers of the World Hockey Association, taking Rookie of the Year honors and setting the hockey world on notice that The Kid was growing up. It would not be long before he was skating in the NHL with the Edmonton Oilers. It took Gretzky and the Oilers several years of steady work, but the leadership skills of Number 99 brought the Alberta squad to the brink of hockey supremacy in 1983, and finally, in 1984, to its first Stanley Cup.

The dominance of the Edmonton Oilers and Wayne Gretzky continued through the 1980s, winning three more Stanley Cups. Late in 1988, the sports world was shocked by

Opposite: *Cliff Whitlow, president of Six Nations Jr. lacrosse team, presents a plaque to Wayne after he signed with the Indianapolis Racers in 1978.*

Left: *Wayne Gretzky with Bernie Nicholls after Nicholls was traded to the Rangers.*

Page 10: *A jubilant Wayne Gretzky celebrates a goal during the 1987 Canada Cup.*

Page 11: *Wayne steals all the silverware that matters at NHL awards banquets: The Stanley, the Art Ross, the Pearson, the Hart, and the Prince of Wales.*

the most unexpected turn of events in the history of ice hockey. Wayne Gretzky's sale to the Los Angeles Kings was among the greatest transactions in professional sports. His future with the Kings may very well include more Stanley Cup wins, but the shift in balance of the western Smythe Division will certainly change the course of many hockey clubs around the National Hockey League.

The story of Wayne Gretzky reads like the NHL Record Book. He has set more than 50 high watermarks in the world's top hockey loop, including highest number of points ever accumulated, most assists, most points in a season, and virtually every record available to a forward player, except those for longevity. He may break those records as well, but only time will tell.

Gretzky has left his imprint on the NHL, but he has also had ample opportunity to display his skills on the world stage. From his first appearance at the World Junior Championships in 1978, through the 1991 Canada Cup, The Great One has consistently shown that his dominance of the hockey scene extends worldwide.

Gretzky is a brilliant playmaker, a consummate goal-scorer, an on-ice leader, and a team player without equal. He is consistent and unceasingly prolific. He is, quite simply, the greatest player ever to play the game of ice hockey.

CHAPTER 1 A STAR IS BORN

Wayne Gretzky was born in 1961 in Brantford, Ontario, a rural hub community in the southwestern part of the province. But the Gretzky story doesn't begin there. To appreciate the world's greatest hockey player, a look into his ancestry is necessary. Tony Gretzky, Wayne's grandfather, had emigrated from Russia as a youth, and his grandmother, Mary, had come to Canada from Poland as a young woman. In the 1930s, they settled in the country just outside of Brantford. Brantford is in the food basket of southern Canada, and they took it upon themselves to fill that food basket with fruits and vegetables. Farming in southern Ontario is a rewarding life, as the soil is rich and the markets are near, but all farming requires patience, hard work, and stubbornness. Fortunately, the Gretzky's had no lack of any of these traits. More fortunately, they were able to pass these qualities along the blood lines.

His father, Walter, spent his working life toiling at a blue collar job at the phone company in Brantford. Wayne gives most of the credit for his success to his dad, who acted as chauffeur, equipment manager, friend, coach and biggest fan to Wayne through all the years of his youth. One might expect Walter to have 'cashed in' once the money tap began to flow. But even after Wayne started making big money, Walter continued to work for the phone company. Wayne could probably have bought the phone company in Brantford, but his dad was happy to get up at the crack of dawn and drive to his job, like most other dads in Brantford. We all know guys like Walter Gretzky: they work hard, they have patience, and they are stubborn. This is as easy to understand as it is to respect.

By the age of two, most children have learned to walk; by that age, the first-born son of Walter and Phyllis Gretzky

Left: *Wayne's father, Walter, clears the snow off Wayne's backyard skating rink.*

Opposite above: *Athletic 10-year-old Gretzky poses here with the tools of his two favorite sports — hockey and lacrosse.*

had learned to skate. By the time Wayne was four years old, Walter had begun the annual process of flooding his backyard for the winter season, thus saving himself the trouble of taking the precocious little skater to the ice rink in the park.

Walter Gretzky was a pretty good hockey player in his youth and continued to play industrial league hockey into his middle age. He was also rather small of stature, so he knew how to play with his head. This was what he passed on to Wayne: play smart, play with heart, and don't give up. Most fathers of five-year-old Canadian boys take them to an ice rink and have them push a chair around the ice until they feel comfortable enough to replace the chair with a stick to help them balance. In Walter's case, his five-year-old could already skate like a 10-year-old, so he set up a training regime that included puck handling, obstacle courses, and target shooting. Walter was blessed with a remarkable little athlete, and he might well have wondered, if only to himself, what a fantastic future might be in store for his pint-sized puck slinger.

When Wayne turned six, he was ready to graduate from the backyard rink. Stories are still told by several Brantford area men of how they used to go to the Gretzky's house and play shinny with Wayne, who was six or seven years younger than most of them. He could skate, shoot and score better than any of them, but for Wayne, it wasn't hockey – it was backyard shinny. Hockey involves wearing a uniform, scoring goals, and winning trophies, and this just wasn't it. Walter's problem was to find a team who would take a six-year-old. In Brantford, as in most places, organized hockey begins with 10-year-old kids.

The gods were smiling on the Gretzky family when somebody at the Brantford Atom League caved in and allowed 'Walter's kid' to try out for a spot on the roster. The Atom League was set up for 10-year-olds who were ready to play at an organized level; they must have figured that giving this guy's kid a tryout would get him off of their backs. It did no such thing.

Wayne made the cut, so having allowed him to try out, they had to allow him to play. Imagine a very small six-year-old kid playing on a team with boys almost twice his age, and you have something of the picture presented to the hockey moms and dads around Brantford in the early 1970s: a half-pint bench warmer whose sweater was five sizes too big, who

Left: *Here's 11-year-old Wayne already demonstrating his puck-handling prowess.*

Opposite: *Gretzky poses with his idol, hockey legend Gordie Howe, in 1972.*

Above: *More than 15 years after the facing page's photo was taken, Gretzky talks at his press conference after smashing Gordie Howe's all-time points record.*

came out on the third string and chased the puck like a hound chases a fox. Wayne's sweater fit so badly that his dad tucked it into his pants on the shooting side, and with that, a tradition had begun.

Wayne did not win MVP that year. He didn't win the scoring title, and nobody asked for his autograph. In fact, aside from the fact that he was nearly half the age of his teammates, he was a pretty average player. He scored one goal, and spent most of his time watching the game from the bench. This first season of hockey may be the only time Wayne was just one of the guys on the team; it didn't take long for his ability to start pulling ahead of the pack.

By the time he was 10 years old, he was not just Wayne Gretzky; he had become a national celebrity, and 'The Great Gretzky.' His picture appeared in newspapers and magazines, and he was frequently profiled on sports broadcasts around the country. Why all the fuss? Mostly, it was due to his incredible scoring ability: at 10 years of age, he had scored 378 goals in the 85-game season, shattering all records by an amazing margin of 238 goals. The Nadrofsky Steelers squad featured another pair of future NHL men: Greg Millen still toils in the cages around NHL rinks, and Len Hatchborn was with the Philadelphia Flyers and Los Angeles Kings in the mid-1980s.

When you arrive at the center of national attention before you have reached your 14th year, it is difficult to keep life in perspective. So powerful were the tensions surrounding his young life that Wayne convinced his parents that it would be in his best interest to move out of Brantford and become lost in Toronto's sea of anonymity.

Opposite: *Proud parents Walter and Phyllis Gretzky look at their own Wayne Gretzky scrapbook.*

The Brantford area hockey scene had begun to divide itself into two camps: those who loved Wayne Gretzky, and those who despised him. Canadians have a peculiar national trait: they are two-faced about success. The hockey moms all loved that their son's team won, but they hated the kid who scored all the goals. The above-ice banners welcomed the wunderkind, but the boos from the stands broke his young heart. The big city of Toronto would allow Wayne to become the star of the Bantam circuit by night, and a regular kid by day. By this point, it must have been pretty clear to Walter and Phyllis Gretzky that their son's future was in the NHL rinks. They sent Wayne to live with a family friend in Toronto, where he could play in the Bantam League.

At 14 years old, The Kid, as he came to be known, was way out of his league. The coaches took one look at him and convinced him that it was not in anybody's interest for him to continue at that level. They sent him up ice to the Junior B

league, where he would bump elbows with burgeoning adults. Wayne signed up with the Toronto Young Nationals with some trepidation. It was one thing for a six-year-old kid to play against gangly 10-year-olds, but quite another for a small pubescent to face full-grown teenagers with 10 years' experience in organized hockey. The Kid scored a pair of markers in the first game and figured that he had been given pretty good advice.

As a freshman with the Nats, Gretzky did very well. His regular season was good enough for the league's Rookie of the Year, while his playoff antics impressed even the greatest skeptics: in 23 games he racked up 73 points, and said good-bye to the Junior B league. This was also the year that Wayne Gretzky made his first appearance in the NHL Guide and Record Book. Each team in the Ontario Hockey League has the right to sponsor teams at the Junior B level. One of the perks of the sponsorship is the ability to call up young prospects for a trial on their rosters. In February 1977, the Peterborough Petes brought up The Kid for the allowed limit of three games. While visiting the Major Junior A loop, The Great One set up three goals before shrinking back to the small time.

The elite Junior A hockey league liked the looks of Wayne Gretzky, and he was drafted third overall by the Sault Sainte Marie Greyhounds. This league was peppered with the future stars of the big league rinks, and though he was only 16 years old, Gretzky was immediately called up to play with the nation's finest prospects.

Again, The Kid was up against bigger, tougher, more seasoned players. He was 5'11", about 155 pounds, and a rookie in all respects except in his incredible natural ability. Gretzky had learned well the lessons Walter had taught him: if there is one thing that allows a skinny kid to survive in a sea of puck-hungry brutes, it's playing with the head. Wayne had learned years before that the place to be is not where the puck is, but where it's going.

This was the year that Gretzky became Number 99. He opened the season as Number 19, but as Gordie Howe's biggest fan, was disappointed that Number 9 was already in use. It had become fashionable in the NHL to take on the big numbers – Phil Esposito and Ken Hodge, for example – so Wayne decided to try on Number 99. His first night as a double-digit hockey player was a three-goal night, and the rest, as they say, is history.

Gretzky had become used to success. He certainly worked hard to achieve it, but nonetheless, he had become accustomed to life apart from the pack. The 1977-78 season with the Greyhounds was no exception. From the start of the season, where he pounded those three goals against the Oshawa Generals, to the closing banquet, where he was presented with both Rookie of the Year and Most Gentlemanly Player awards, he gave evidence that he was more ready for big league hockey than his young body allowed. His point total at the close of the season was 182, with 70 goals. Although these numbers were good enough to smash the Junior A record of 170 points, the title was earned by Ottawa's beloved Bobby Smith, who beat Gretzky to the punch by racking up the till for 192 points on the season.

Wayne Gretzky, scholastic pursuits aside, had graduated again, and now he was ready for the biggest challenge of his on-ice career.

CHAPTER 2 THE EDMONTON YEARS

At the age of 17, there was only one place for Gretzky to pursue his dream of playing professional hockey: the World Hockey Association. Long-time family friend and agent Gus Badali, after numerous conversations with Wayne and his family, began to search for the right opportunity for the young phenomenon to ply his trade. The Birmingham Bulls expressed some interest, but were unwilling to make the kind of financial deal Badali was after.

Word on the hockey grapevine suggested that entrepreneur Nelson Skalbania was willing to make the Gretzky family an offer they couldn't refuse. A businessman with a keen eye for investment opportunities, Skalbania would never be mistaken for a hockey expert. But neither was he a fool. On instinct, and against the advice of knowledgeable hockey men, Skalbania was able to make one of the wisest investments of his career. He had only seen Gretzky skate on paper, but he'd taken him on an arduous jog around Vancouver and was impressed with Wayne's athletic ability, in sneakers at least. He offered Gretzky a four-year package worth almost a million dollars.

Skalbania, who owned the Indianapolis Racers WHA franchise, hadn't seen Gretzky actually play the game, but on Wayne's word and an endorsement from former Houston Aeros coach Bill Dineen, he signed him to a personal services contract and sent him to start his pro career in Indiana, not exactly a hotbed of hockey.

Left: *Nelson Skalbania, owner of the Indianapolis Racers, signs the 17-year-old kid to a seven year pro contract.*

Opposite left: *The soon-to-be Great One with his first pro team, the WHA's Indianapolis Racers.*

Opposite right: *In 1979 Gretzky and Eddie Mio were sold to the Edmonton Oilers of the WHA.*

Gretzky had a slow start, compiling six points in eight games, totals that failed to rouse any response in the dwindling hockey population of Indianapolis. When Skalbania saw that Gretzky's obvious talents could only deliver dividends in a location with paying customers, he arranged to sell The Kid, along with Eddie Mio and Peter Driscoll, to Peter Pocklington, owner of the WHA Edmonton Oilers. Pocklington immediately began negotiations to sign Wayne to a 10-year deal worth three million dollars, again without ever seeing Wayne play the game. Included in the deal was an option for another 10 years. Although Gretzky was not happy about the length of the arrangement and its ramifications, he inked the contract on his 18th birthday at center ice at Northlands Coliseum on January 26, 1979. That contract would change Gretzky's life in more ways than he could have imagined.

Gretzky's first year in professional hockey was a preview of his future. Ignoring the abuse of fans, the scepticism of hockey mandarins and critical pens of a doubting press, he just played hockey. The highlight of his rookie campaign came when he was able to line up beside his childhood hero and mentor, Gordie Howe, in the WHA All-Star Game. Howe, who had been watching The Kid progress throughout the season, proved that his eye was as accurate as ever when assessing young talent. Mr. Hockey predicted that if, and when, Gretzky made it to the NHL, the marks he established in his own quarter of a century would soon vanish.

By season's end, Gretzky had convinced his WHA peers that he could deliver the goods. Counting his eight games with Indianapolis, Gretzky recorded 46 goals and 64 assists

for a total of 104 points, good for fifth place on the scoring parade and the WHA Rookie of the Year award.

With The Great One aboard, the Oilers finished in first place, leading the league in goals scored and goals against. Gretzky led the squad in goals, assists and points, outscoring his nearest teammate by 34 points. The Oilers' pipeline continued to flow into the WHA playoffs, eliminating New England in a tough seven-game battle which earned them the right to play the Winnipeg Jets for the WHA's biggest prize, the Avco Cup. The youthful Oilers were no match for the older, experienced Jets, as Winnipeg flew past Edmonton in six games. Gretzky, however, showed he was not intimidated by his first taste of post-season action as a professional. He led all playoff scorers in goals and in points – not bad for an 18-year-old not yet old enough to drink or vote.

In March 1979, the NHL and the WHA announced that they had reached an agreement for a merger/expansion. Four of the existing WHA squads – Winnipeg, New England, Quebec and Edmonton – would join the National Hockey League. The NHL lowered its draft age to 18, thereby allowing under-age juniors who had signed WHA contracts to play in the new 21-team league. In the complicated expansion draft of 1979, the Oilers had first to reclaim Gretzky as an under-age junior, then protect him as a priority choice.

Finally, with his entry into the NHL, the rest of the hockey world would be able to see The Great Gretzky for themselves. Only a handful of dedicated hockey fans had followed the fortunes of the WHA, but the NHL was 'the bigs.'

There were still critics who were ready to dismiss him as a flash in the pan, the most vocal being New York sportswriter Stan Fischler, who hadn't been able to watch hockey with an open mind since Bobby Orr retired.

The NHL dictated that any player who performed in the WHA would not be considered a rookie in the expanded NHL, thereby robbing Gretzky of the opportunity to set any rookie marks that counted. Regardless of his prior experience, at the age of 18, he was certainly a newcomer to the level of play that greeted him when he made his NHL debut. It was a tougher game than he had ever faced. Guided by his keen ability to see the game from all angles, he quickly adapted to the faster play and stronger opponents.

Though he started slow, it was hard to hide his light under a bushel, and he was given the nod to play in the 1980 All-Star Game in Detroit. The talents of The Great Gretzky were showcased in Motown, where he would be elbow to elbow with Detroit's very own Gordie Howe, who at the age of 51 was back in the NHL with the Hartford (New England) Whalers.

Twenty points behind Marcel Dionne in the scoring race after 50 games, Gretzky caught the Los Angeles Kings star with three games remaining. On April 2, 1980, Gretzky became the youngest player ever to score 50 goals in a season. As pleased as he was with the record, he was more enthusiastic about the play of his team, who won nine of its last 10 games to finish with 69 points and clinch a playoff berth. When the curtain fell on his first NHL campaign, Gretzky and Dionne were neck and neck in the Art Ross race. Dionne, having scored more goals (though fewer assists) was awarded the title and the Art Ross Trophy. Wayne led the loop with 86 assists, a category he has never let slip through his fingers. Gretzky's disappointment at missing out on the scoring crown was tempered with the Hart and

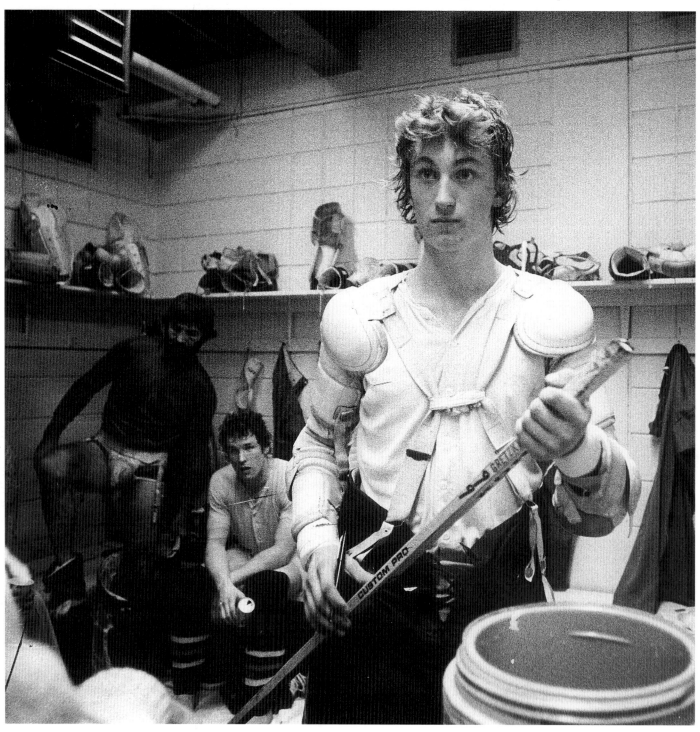

Opposite: *Gretzky after his last WHA game, May 20, 1979.*

Above: *Gretzky during the 1983 Cup finals.*

Right: *Gordie Howe, one of the first NHL stars to acknowledge Gretzky's abilities, shares an accolade with Wayne at the 1980 All-Star Game.*

Lady Byng trophies, the first of what would be a virtual torrent of individual NHL accolades.

The Oilers' first playoff appearance was a brief one, losing three straight games to the eventual Stanley Cup finalists, the Philadelphia Flyers. The series was closer than the sweep would indicate, however. The Oilers lost two overtime matches to the Flyers, including a double overtime defeat in the decisive third match. Gretzky managed three points in the three games.

With a strong supporting cast that included Mark Messier, Glenn Anderson, Kevin Lowe and newcomers Jari Kurri and Paul Coffey, the Oilers finished in fourth place in the Smythe Division in 1980-81, just four points out of second spot. Gretzky won the scoring title outright, breaking Bobby Orr's record for assists and adding another Hart Trophy to his growing collection of silverware.

The 1980-81 playoffs gave the first indication that this young group of athletes from the oil fields of Alberta would soon be a force to be reckoned with. In the first round, the Oilers met the Montreal Canadiens, as storied a sports franchise as has ever existed. The Oilers didn't merely win this series – they destroyed the Montrealers, winning the opening two matches at the Forum by convincing 6-3 and 3-1 scores, then applying the knock-out punch at the North-

Left: *Gretzky with the two men who helped him to the top of the NHL: Jari Kurri and Paul Coffey.*

Below left: *Wayne interviewing the toughest man in the league: Mark Messier.*

Opposite: *It's not often that a hockey player makes the cover of* Sports Illustrated. *In 1982 he was named its Sportsman of the Year.*

lands Coliseum with a 6-2 shelling of the 22-time Stanley Cup champions. Gretzky registered five assists in the opening match, the first of many post-season records, and scored a hat-trick in the clinching game. Perhaps more than any victory in Oilers' history, this third game proved that the Oilers, with Number 99 as their offensive catalyst, were destined to make a place for themselves in the Stanley Cup record book.

The fairy tale Oilers were shocked back to reality when they met the defending Cup champion New York Islanders. The young squad didn't fold under the Islanders' relentless attack, and extended the series to six games. As for The Great One, he had an outstanding post-season, racking up seven goals and 14 assists in only nine games, an indication of playoff performances to come.

The 1981-82 season was the year that Wayne Gretzky re-wrote the NHL Guide and Record Book, sending even the stingiest of hockey historians to the bookstore to replace their now badly out of date copies. Gretzky set a plethora of new scoring marks: 50 goals in 39 games, 10 games with at least three goals, 92 goals on the season, a new assists mark and an unheard-of 212 points total. It was an awesome display of sporting prowess, which brought him to the forefront of attention in Canada and eventually to the covers of *Time* magazine and *Sports Illustrated* in the United States. His unassailable crushing of the NHL high watermarks brought him respect both inside and outside the hockey world and earned him the coveted American Press Athlete of the Year Award. This is heady stuff for a 21-year-old. Number 99 was heading to the playoffs with a full head of steam, and a size 99 hat. He was in the big leagues now, though, and he was about to learn a big league lesson: humility.

Left: *Gretzky (99) and Paul Coffey (7, seated) look drained and dejected as the Islanders put icing on the cake in their 1983 sweep of the final series.*

Opposite: *Billy Smith and the New York Islanders held The Great One scoreless through 11 consecutive Stanley Cup final games.*

The 1981-82 Oilers were a devastating scoring machine, blasting 417 pucks behind enemy goaltenders to become the first NHL team to score 400 goals in a single season. They also captured their first Smythe Division regular-season crown, racking up 48 wins and 111 points. They cruised into the playoffs, a cocky, arrogant group of youngsters, overly confident that they could crush any playoff pretenders who stood in their way.

The Oilers' opponent in this first round was the Los Angeles Kings, a team that allowed 55 more goals than it scored and who finished a full 48 points behind the Oilers. However, the Kings had a benchload of seasoned NHL veterans, including Marcel Dionne, Dave Taylor and Jimmy Fox. After surprising Edmonton in the first game by out-slugging them 10-8, the Kings lost a close 3-2 overtime decision in the second match and fell behind the Oilers 5-0 in the third game of the best-of-five set.

The Kings watched stoically as the Oilers high-fived each other after the fifth goal, strutting their certain victory and berating the Kings for such a shoddy effort. Rumor has it the Oilers were so busy planning a 'night on the town' victory party in the City of Angels that they barely noticed that the Kings were beginning the greatest comeback in their 15-year existence until it was too late.

History tells us the Kings fired six unanswered goals to win that match 6-5 in overtime, then went on to capture the series three games to two in one of the NHL's greatest upsets. History also tells us that while individuals win scoring titles, teams win Stanley Cups. From this moment on, the Edmonton Oilers would be a team.

Entering the 1982-83 season, the Oilers were determined to prove they had learned something they couldn't learn on the dressing room chalkboard: teamsmanship. They set a new NHL mark by pasting 424 goals in the 80-game season. Although his goal total fell from 92 to 71, Gretzky left the banquet with the Art Ross Trophy again. He established another assists mark, setting up his teammates a record 125 times.

The Kid was a goal-scoring machine, but he was taking home all the silverware except the one that really matters in hockey. He realized that if the Oilers were to get past strong, consistent teams like the Islanders, they had to create a well-tuned team, and spread out the attack evenly across their forward lines. With most opposing teams concentrating on stopping him, he could dish the puck off to his forwards, meaning they could reap the benefits individually and the team could prosper collectively.

It was a game plan that was hard to dismiss. The Oilers had four players with at least 100 points: Gretzky, Anderson, Messier and Kurri. Paul Coffey, in only his third NHL season, proved himself to be the league's finest offensive rearguard, finishing just below the 100 mark with 96 points. Edmonton captured its second Smythe crown and sailed into the post-season, confident but wisely cautious.

The Oilers cruised through the preliminary rounds, losing just one game. Their attack was awesome, mixing ex-plosive offense with stingy defense. In the quarterfinals against Calgary, they scored 35 goals in five games; in the semifinals against Chicago, they allowed just 11 goals in four games.

Gretzky was running on high-test fuel, scoring a dozen goals and assisting on 22 others in only 12 games. When the Oilers gushed past the Blackhawks in four straight, they arrived on the Stanley Cup doorstep, fully primed and precision tuned.

Unfortunately, their opponents were the three-time Stanley Cup champion New York Islanders, and they were about to give their western pupils a lesson in Stanley Cup hockey. The Islanders neutralized Gretzky perfectly, holding him to only four assists in four games as they swept Edmonton out of the Stanley Cup money in straight games. The Islanders were masters of playing 'the game within the game,' using every psychological edge known to upset the Oilers' rhythm. Battlin' Billy Smith feigned injury every time an Oiler came near his crease. His dramatics were the source of several unearned Oiler penalties, and a lesson Gretzky would absorb.

The Islanders won every game by at least a two-goal margin.

Although Gretzky led all scorers in the post-season, the Islanders threw a defensive blanket over him. The crafty veterans shut down Gretzky's offensive skills and frustrated him to the point where he lost his best weapon: his cool under pressure. Operating their hold over Gretzky with the precision of a surgeon, the Isles held The Great One scoreless and he agonized over the thought that if he had been able to pop just one timely marker, perhaps the series would have turned around. However, the truth is, as far as the Oilers had come and as good as they were, they weren't good enough – yet.

The Edmonton Oilers always envisioned themselves as the new breed of hockey franchise. It was a team built on speed and offensive wizardry who worked so well together as a unit that, despite its defensive liabilities, could march into the winner's circle on the strength of its offense alone.

They had learned something from their also-ran performances. Coach Glen Sather knew that to win a Stanley Cup he had to prepare them more efficiently as a defensive unit, but he also knew that their overpowering fore-checking and creative power play units would force the opposition into mistakes. When the opportunities were created, the goal scorers would be there, led by or fed by Wayne Gretzky.

Never has professional hockey seen an offensive display like the show put on by the 1983-84 Edmonton Oilers. Wayne Gretzky, of course, was the catalyst, returning to the top of the leader board by netting 87 goals, the second-highest goal total in history, and breaking the 200-point barrier for the second time. The Oilers had three players with 50 goals or more: The Kid, his Finnish protégé Jari Kurri and the young master, Glenn Anderson. They exploded out of the blocks, firing 446 pucks through, around and under

enemy netminders, an incredible 5.58 average per game. If that wasn't enough, they scored a league record 36 short-handed goals, proving once again that the best defense is a great offense. They won a franchise-high 57 games and finished first overall in the league for the first time. In the 1984 playoffs, all post-season roads led directly to the Northlands Coliseum.

The Oilers' surge to the 1984 Stanley Cup finals was rougher than the path they had traveled in 1983. They easily disposed of the Winnipeg Jets, but needed seven games to snuff out the stubborn Calgary Flames before sweeping past the Minnesota North Stars. The Oilers reached the Stanley Cup finals with a return ticket to fight the New York Islanders, who were counting on their fifth straight Stanley Cup victory. This year, however, the pupils became the teachers, outclassing the Islanders by beating them at their own game.

The Oilers, much to the surprise of every armchair quarterback and the 18,000 screaming denizens in Northlands Coliseum, played Game One tight to the vest, shutting down the Islanders' attack through two stanzas and making Kevin McClelland's power play marker in the third period stand up in a 1-0 nailbiter. Although, as a unit, the Oilers were flowing, Wayne Gretzky had a personal curse to overcome. He still hadn't been able to score a post-season goal against the Islanders, a drought that eventually reached 12 games.

With the Oilers leading two games to one, The Great One finally broke off his most agonizing slump and, as usual, he did it with a vengeance. He fired a brace of goals in the final two contests and the Oilers disposed of the Islanders in five games. Wayne Gretzky had doubters: there were still those who vowed that he would go the way of Hall of Famers Bill

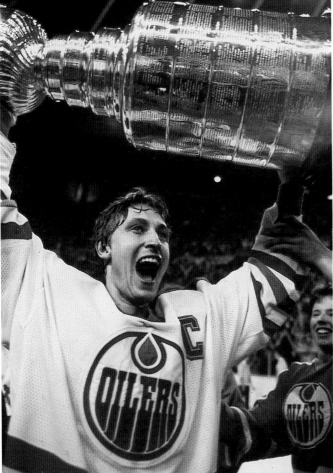

Opposite: *Number 99 with Jari Kurri.*

Above: *Skating the line in the '84 Cup finals.*

Left: *In 1984 the dream comes true: Stanley Cup Champs!*

Overleaf: *Wayne Gretzky in action during the Stanley Cup finals.*

Gadsby, Harry Howell, Rod Gilbert and Brad Park and play a remarkable career without savoring a Stanley Cup win. But in true storybook fashion, Prince Charming came home with the silverware.

Another side of the man comes out of this happy ending. Gretzky has often said that beyond the joy of winning Lord Stanley's coveted Mug, his happiest moment was seeing Mark Messier win the Conn Smythe Trophy as the playoff MVP. Gretzky knew that the heart and soul of the Oilers' franchise was Mark Messier, an Edmonton native with a heart as big as his threshold for pain, and Gretzky was proud that Mess's sizable contribution to the Oilers' victory was recognized.

Of course, now that they had ascended to the throne, it was up to the Oilers to defend it. Riding on the coattails of the Gretzky-Kurri express, the 1984-85 Oilers easily repeated as Smythe Division crown holders. Although their overall goal totals were down, they still victimized opposing defenses 401 times. Paul Coffey became the third defenseman to record 100 points in a season, and Gretzky, with 73 goals and a record-setting 135 assists, won his fourth Art Ross Trophy. With Grant Fuhr establishing himself as the Oilers' number one pivot by winning 26 games and losing only eight, the Oilers were prepared to defend the Mug.

Above left: *Before Gretzky, hockey was played from the goal crease out; how things have changed. . . .*

Below left: *Gretzky is interviewed during the 1985 Cup final. He is holding his younger brother Brent.*

Opposite left: *Tying up Gretzky can be a costly maneuver. The Flyers found this out the hard way in the 1985 final series.*

Opposite right: *99 and 66: Wayne Gretzky and Mario Lemieux.*

In post-season play, Gretzky set another mark, this time picking up 47 points in 18 playoff games as the Oilers cruised into the Stanley Cup winner's circle again. His playoff romp began with a seven-point parade in Winnipeg on April 25th, and continued into the semifinals against Chicago. Gretzky astonished even himself by picking up 18 points in six games. He scored four goals himself and gift-wrapped 14 others as the Oilers set a league record with 44 goals in the six-game set.

In the finals, the Philadelphia Flyers had the misfortune of meeting an Oilers squad poised to repeat as champions. Although the Flyers jumped on Edmonton with a 4-1 win in Game One, the Oilers struck gold in the next four games, sweeping the remaining encounters to earn their second consecutive Stanley Cup victory. In the pivotal third game, Gretzky scored three first-period goals to ice a 4-3 Edmonton win. In the decisive fifth match, with the outcome still very much in question, Gretzky potted a pair of second-frame markers and the Oilers coasted to a 8-3 win. The selection committee had no problem picking the playoff MVP, and Wayne Gretzky earned the one piece of silverware missing from his trophy shelf – the Conn Smythe Trophy.

With the fans clamoring for a 'three-peat,' the Oilers entered the 1986 season under considerable expectations. They opened the spigot for the regular season, adding another Smythe Division banner for their home rink. Three of the top four scorers wore Oilers colors, with The Great One registering a career-high 215 points. Paul Coffey scored 48 goals from his office on the blueline, the most by a rearguard in the history of the game. The Oilers once again featured three 50-goal marksmen, the same trio who put their names in the record book in 1984. However, as was the case in Gretzky's other record-stirring season, the ultimate prize escaped their grasp.

After easing past the Vancouver Canucks in straight games, the Oilers met the Calgary Flames in the quarterfinals. The series, one of the most exciting in recent years, was undecided after six closely fought matches. In the third

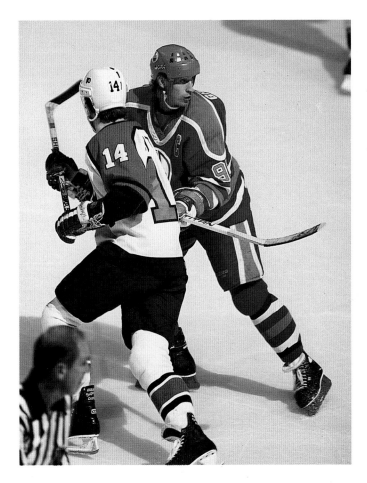

period of the decisive seventh game, with the teams squared at two's, Oilers defenseman Steve Smith picked up a loose puck behind the Oilers' cage and fired a pass across the crease that hit Grant Fuhr's leg and trickled across the line. The Flames capitalized on the Smith error, making the un-earned goal stand up as the series-winning marker.

Although the Oilers, to a man, refused to blame Smith's errant pass, the fans weren't quite so forgiving. Gretzky was on a roll with 19 points in 10 games, but he would have to fight and win another NHL season before being allowed another spin at the Stanley Cup table.

The 1987 Oilers were still the dominating offensive squad in the league, and although they failed to reach the 400-goal mark for the first time in five seasons, the 372 pucks that did cross opposition goal lines was enough to lead the league. Again, three of the top four scorers were Oilers, with Mark Messier making his first appearance at the top of the rank-ing. Still, the season was played under the shadow of their 1986 failure.

Revenge for the 1986 playoff spanking may have been the primary motivating force behind the Oilers' drive in the 1987 campaign, though there is a natural and good-natured rivalry between residents of Calgary and Edmonton. The regular season saw tireless battles between the interpro-vincial rivals, but they never got the chance to carry it into the playoffs. The Flames, guilty of looking down the road before they hit the highway, were unceremoniously removed from the post-season by the Winnipeg Jets. The Oilers coolly accepted their good fortune and romped into the Stanley Cup finals for the fourth time in five seasons. The improved Philadelphia Flyers provided the opposition.

Edmonton should have won this series easily, taking a two-game lead compliments of Gretzky, who opened the scoring in each of the first two contests. After losing Game Three, Edmonton took a 3-1 lead in games with a 4-1 win at

the Spectrum. However, the Oilers still had demons to ex-orcise. They blew 3-1 and 2-0 leads in Games Five and Six to force a seventh game. With the score tied at 1-1, Gretzky maneuvered into the Flyers' zone and looped a perfect pass to his favorite target, Jari Kurri, who slammed home the Cup-winning goal.

Amid the hoopla on the ice following the final whistle, Captain Gretzky searched out Steve Smith, and in front of millions of TV viewers and the Northlands Coliseum faith-ful, gave Smith the Cup to hold high and proud, easing the bitter memories that had plagued the young defenseman for 13 months.

Gretzky finished atop the post-season scoring ladder again, and although he only potted five playoff goals, he assisted on seven of the Oilers' last 12 goals in the finals.

Wayne Gretzky and the Oilers found themselves in un-familiar territory in 1988. For the first time in seven seasons, they failed to repeat as Smythe Division leaders, and for the first time since 1980, Wayne Gretzky failed to win the Art Ross Trophy. The Oilers were unseated by the Calgary Flames and The Great One was upstaged by Mario 'The Magnificent' Lemieux. Gretzky, who missed 16 games due to injury, did manage to set the all-time NHL record for assists, the proudest moment of his NHL career.

After playing into late May in the 1987 Stanley Cup finals and playing most of the summer in the Canada Cup, Gretz-ky's injuries couldn't have come at a better time. It gave him time to refuel and concentrate on the post-season, a playoff year in which the Edmonton Oilers were going to be decided underdogs.

Whoever was making the line on odds for an Oilers repeat either underestimated the power of Wayne Gretzky's com-mitment to excellence or just didn't know the game. When the bell rang to begin the 1988 playoffs, Gretzky shot out of the starting gate, leaving the field eating dust.

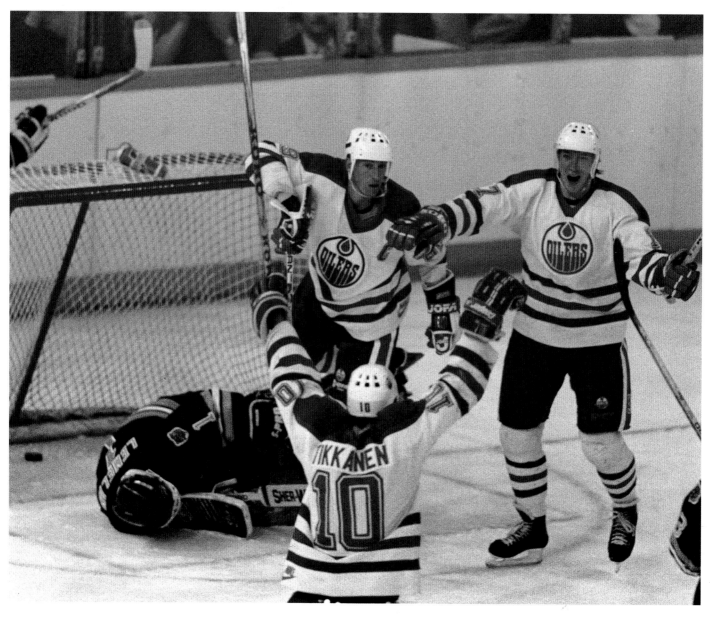

The return bout between the Oilers and Flames finally materialized in the western round of the 1988 playoffs. However, this slugfest was a mismatch that was over in four quick games. Although the scores were close, the Flames never had a chance against the boiling Oilers. After the Oilers sneaked out a win in the first tilt, the teams were battling in overtime in Game Two when Edmonton was called for a penalty, giving the Flames a perfect chance to get back in the series. Midway through the Flames' power play, Gretzky grabbed a loose puck and broke down the wing, unleashing a slapshot just as he crossed the blueline. Mike Vernon, surprised at both the shot selection and its velocity, could only watch as the disc flew over his shoulder, giving the Oilers the victory and a commanding lead they would never surrender. In hindsight, Gretzky calls that goal the most important of his career, a fitting example of his commitment to team goals and performance.

With the Flames burned out, Gretzky and the Oilers set their sights on the Boston Bruins, who were aroused from a decade of Stanley Cup hibernation. Unfortunately for the Bears, their den was about to be invaded by a revitalized Wayne Gretzky.

In an awesome display of post-season dramatics, Gretzky virtually knocked the Bruins out all by himself, racking up a record 13 points in the finals, including a record 10 assists.

Even divine intervention failed to halt the Oilers express. Midway through the fourth contest, a power failure turned the lights out on the game. All it did was delay the inevitable and give Gretzky another 60 minutes to work his magic. With 43 points in only 19 games, Gretzky won the Conn Smythe Trophy, ensuring that he wouldn't be shut out of the hardware at the NHL Awards banquet.

The Oilers, in solid Stanley Cup tradition, paraded the Cup around the ice. This was their fourth Stanley Cup, and they were exercising their bragging rights. This wasn't just a hockey team, this was a family. Gretzky called all his teammates together – the skaters, non-starters, trainers, coaches and executives – and sat them at center ice for a Stanley Cup family portrait. It was a fitting, and as fate would have it, ironic gesture of team spirit that has become a Stanley Cup tradition.

The faces in the Edmonton Oilers yearbook today are very different from those of that night of triumph. They have been replaced by capable players who maintain the Oilers' high regard for professional product. All teams change, but no one in his right mind could have foreseen the Edmonton Oilers without Number 99. No matter where they play, or how successful they become, the Edmonton Oilers will always be known as the team that traded Wayne Gretzky, the greatest athlete to ever play a team sport.

Opposite: *The Boston Bruins were toppled by the Oilers in four straight in 1988. Here Reg Lemelin is beat by the Gretzky, Kurri, Tikkanen line.*

Right: *In 1988, the Oilers took their fourth Stanley Cup.*

Below: *A tradition in the making. This on-ice Cup pose has become an annual obligation.*

CHAPTER 3 THE DEAL OF THE CENTURY

Though they were elated by his continuous stream of re-markable achievements, Gretzky watchers could be forgiven for losing track of his career. He had become the most celebrated person in Canada, was widely known throughout the world, and had turned all positive predictions of his life and career into concrete reality. So numerous and constant were his successes, the remarkable had become predictable. It would not be long, however, before The Great One's career would startle the sports world and bring new life to the pages of Canadian journals.

For Gretzky, it was a time of introspection. He had realized more of his boyhood dreams than anyone has a right to achieve, but he was 26 years old, and his personal life was showing signs of the grind. His long-standing relationship with Edmonton entertainer Vicki Moss was coming to a close – she had moved to Los Angeles to pursue a career as a singer – and his 20 years in the public eye was wearing him down.

While on vacation in southern California, he and a friend, Alan Thicke, drove into Los Angeles to take in a Lakers game at the Great Western Forum. It could never have occurred to The Kid that the drive to L.A. would usher in an entirely new chapter in his life.

Gretzky had met Janet Jones several times over the years. She had been involved with athletes and actors, and their paths had crossed at parties and sporting events. This time, when he bumped into her at the Lakers game, he was single, she was single, and sparks were flying. Nobody remembers who won the game that night, but for Wayne Gretzky, Janet Jones, and the entire hockey community, it marked the beginning of some very big changes.

Janet Jones was an actress, dancer, model, and Nouveau American socialite. As an actress, she was not exactly Meryl Streep, but she had turned in respectable performances in middle-of-the-road films, had danced at the Radio City Music Hall in New York, and was recognized as a fashion model of renown. Like Wayne, she had grown up in a middle-class family, had achieved early successes in her life, and lived the fast-paced life of an entertainment profesional. She had also just emerged from a long-term relationship, hers with tennis star Vitas Geruliatis.

On January 10, 1988, after getting her mother's go-ahead, Wayne Gretzky proposed marriage to Janet Jones. By week's end, the Canadian public knew more about Janet Jones than they knew about the Queen of England. The wedding would be in July of that year, and it would be the event of the decade.

They called it 'The Royal Wedding' in most of the papers. For weeks the daily press was full of tidbits of gossip on everything from the cost of Janet's Pari Malek original wedding gown to the gritty details of the guest list for the country's social event of the season. Canada was sizing up their hero's bride-to-be at water coolers and taverns from coast to coast. Frankly, she had several strikes against her. First, she was American; second, she had made a demure appearance in *Playboy* magazine, and third, she was just too beautiful to be a 'nice girl.' In the end, Canada welcomed Janet Jones, but it was a rough road for the southern belle who would become 'The First Lady of Ice Hockey.'

When, on July 16th, Wayne and Janet Gretzky emerged from St. Joseph's Basilica in Edmonton, they were greeted by thousands of well-wishers. The streets were jammed for blocks with hockey fans, gawkers and the world press corps. Wayne and Janet performed the post-nuptial kisses to the delight of the cheering crowd and photo editors everywhere. Music blared into the street as millionaires, puckshooters, movie stars and politicians mingled on the steps before filtering into their waiting cars.

Opposite: *Janet Jones, American actress and model, became the leading lady in Wayne's life.*

Right: *Wayne and Janet Jones with Stanley.*

Below: *Mr. and Mrs. Wayne Gretzky during their wedding extravaganza.*

It was billed as the 'Wedding of the Century,' and so it was received. National television covered the event from every possible angle. Canadians loved him, or loved to hate him, but he was a national institution. As a nation, Canada was having serious identity problems, but one of the few things they all agreed on was the importance of Gretzky as a symbol of national pride. The advent of free trade with the United States had left many Canadians feeling threatened, but there was one thing the country could count on: Wayne Gretzky.

It was against this backdrop that the next scene in the life of Wayne Gretzky was played. Understanding the national psyche is a prerequisite to understanding the wailing and gnashing of teeth which greeted his departure from the Canadian stage.

Wayne and Janet Gretzky were only six days into their honeymoon when Wayne received a phone call at Janet's apartment in Los Angeles. The call was from Bruce McNall, owner of the Los Angeles Kings. McNall announced to a very surprised newlywed that he had been given permission by Peter Pocklington to speak to The Kid about a future playing hockey in California. Wayne was surprised, and hurt. He was not surprised that he was being offered for sale, but rather because Pocklington had not first called Wayne himself. This would seem to be the beginning of the biggest sale in the history of the game; but the truth of the matter is, the sale of The Great One was inevitable.

Wayne had recently come to financial terms with Pocklington in a contract that gave Gretzky his freedom after five years. He was the greatest player ever, but he was reaching

Left: *Bruce McNall, owner of the L.A. Kings, brought Gretzky to the City of Angels.*

Below: *Peter Pocklington, the man who sold The Great One.*

Opposite: *The sale of Wayne Gretzky to the Los Angeles Kings was the most spectacular transaction in modern sports.*

his peak. If he was to be profitably dealt, it would have to be while he was at his best, and while there was still a reasonable amount of time left in the contract. It would be difficult to sell an aging superstar with only a year or two left in his agreement, so Pocklington started shopping The Kid around the league.

Properties like Wayne Gretzky don't come along every day, so Pocklington had little trouble finding interested buyers. The first offer came from Nelson Skalbania, who had sold Wayne's personal services contract to Peter Pocklington 10 years earlier. This deal would have seen Wayne go to Vancouver, British Columbia, to play with the Canucks. Pocklington would get his badly needed cash, while Gretzky would get cash and a big piece of the Vancouver franchise.

The Kid got word of this cozy deal only hours after winning his fourth Stanley Cup in five years. Having realized the truth of the trade rumors, he got busy making a deal of his own.

The deal seems to have been that Pocklington would allow Wayne to choose his destination, and in return, Wayne would take the heat. There would be heat, and Pocklington would feel it: Wayne Gretzky had become the number one Canadian national treasure, and was the favorite son of Edmonton fans. With serious interests in the oil, meat, milk, used car and sports markets in Alberta, Pocklington had reason to fear a backlash. A boycott could affect his sales of everything from milk shakes to Mustangs. In retrospect, Gretzky got the best of this deal by a wide mar-

gin. He got money, a home of his choice, and a fresh start in a great hockey town. Pocklington ended up with a national black eye that may never heal, despite Gretzky's determined attempts to bear the responsibility like a penitent sinner.

The call from Bruce McNall may have surprised The Kid, but Wayne had met McNall on a few occasions, and he liked him. When McNall suggested that they talk over Wayne's future at a private dinner, a date was set, and the deal was in the works.

McNall has a reputation in sports and business circles: he's known as a big shooter with horseshoes in his hip pocket. The very model of the American-Dream-come-true, McNall was a serious numismatic enthusiast and coin dealer from the age of 15, and has been turning old coins into new money ever since. He has financial holdings in coins and antiques, film production, horse breeding and professional sports teams. When, in 1988, McNall made that call to Wayne Gretzky, he was 37 years old and worth more than $100 million. He had made a career of making impossible things happen, and he was determined to pull a Kings jersey over the head of the Crown Prince of hockey.

With his new wife Janet having an established life in Glittertown, Los Angeles seemed to be a natural place for The Kid to settle. He would gain the anonymity he had craved since boyhood, the support of a very respectable hockey team, the chance to build a franchise from the inside out, and distance from Peter Pocklington. McNall could have driven a hard bargain, but from all reports, Gretzky wrote his own ticket. If Peter Pocklington slunk out of the deal looking like the cat that swallowed the canary, McNall strode into the future with the air of an American Prometheus, bringing fire to the Los Angeles ice.

The basic deal McNall and Gretzky arranged was as follows: Pocklington would get $15 million cash, the Oilers received two of the Kings' most promising skaters, Jimmy Carson and Martin Gelinas, and three first round draft picks. McNall would take home three Oilers: Marty McSorley, Mike Krushelnyski, and Wayne Gretzky. Gretzky would move into his new home on the coast five million dollars richer, and with a brand new lucrative playing contract. Although very few people knew it at the time, Wayne Gretzky became a Los Angeles King in July 1988.

This was the biggest deal in the history of ice hockey, and one of the most remarkable ever in professional sports. It didn't take long for leaks to develop. By the first week of August NHL fax machines were full of rumors; something was in the wind and it involved Wayne Gretzky. On August 9th a press conference was called in Edmonton and the world took notice. Once again, Number 99 was front page news across Canada and the United States.

Stateside, the deal was big news and good news. The entry of Wayne Gretzky, arguably the biggest superstar in professional sports, could bring new sparkle to Tinseltown. NHL owners were delighted with the high profile Gretzky would bring to the game in the American market, and major sponsors began lining up to exploit the new-found status of the Los Angeles Kings.

In Canada, the news was received rather differently. The first reaction in the Great White North was shock. It was not long before shock turned to outrage. The first target for the bubbling Canadian ire was Janet Jones. Hockey fans from Come-by-chance to Nanaimo had decided that this 'Delilah' had done to the greatest team in hockey what Yoko Ono had done to the Beatles.

It wasn't long before the search for a villain centered on Peter Pocklington. Janet Jones had been found not-guilty in the kangaroo court that is the popular press, and Peter Pocklington was the most obvious target for the rage of an offended populace. Pocklington denied ever wanting to trade his protégé, insisting that the deal was Wayne's idea, and that he'd only been looking after the expressed wishes of the man who had brought him four Stanley Cups. Almost nobody bought the Pocklington/Gretzky version of events. The obvious financial gain for Pocklington, coupled with his

comments in the days following the trade, convinced the press and public that Wayne had been sold out.

With time and subsequent Oiler triumphs, the venom of hockey fans and nationalists has dissipated somewhat. The Great Hockey Sale has been accepted as a cold business decision, and though Canadians may not be terribly forgiving, they are known as a people who accept reality on its own terms. Some still blame Janet Jones, most blame Peter Pocklington, and they blame each other. Through it all, Peter Puck, as Pocklington was known, stuck to his story: Wayne asked to be traded.

Back in Los Angeles, Wayne Gretzky had some work to do. He was no longer among his close friends and team-mates, he had only been married two months, he had moved from a small northern city to the western capital of North America, and, he soon discovered, he was to become a father. He also had a new job, and as the world's most celebrated hockey player, fitting into the new situation would be an exciting problem to face.

Below: *With the trade deal completed, Wayne and Janet are all smiles.*

Opposite: *Wayne Gretzky: The newest King.*

CHAPTER 4 KING GRETZKY

When Gretzky arrived in L.A., the Kings were a team with potential. Their forward squad was their strong suit. Luc Robitaille, the 1987 NHL Rookie of the Year, and sharpshooter Bernie Nicholls led the lineup, with Bobby Carpenter and Dave Taylor still capable of holding their own at an awards banquet. The Kings' weakness was from the blueline back. Although Jay Wells, Tim Watters and Steve Duchesne were all respectable backliners, a slim playmaker like Gretzky would have liked to have had Paul Coffey to pair with his former Oiler-mate Marty McSorley.

Left: *Gretzky in action for his new team.*

Opposite above: *Gretzky, sporting the captain's "C" on his uniform, awaits his turn on the ice.*

Opposite below: *Gretzky with fellow Canadian Michael J. Fox and Kings owner Bruce McNall.*

It only got worse from the blueline in. Since the days when Rogie Vachon patrolled the crease for L.A., they had shuffled through a whole deck of goaltending jokers.

Gretzky's job in Los Angeles was to win hockey games, but the grind of the 80-game schedule was still eight weeks away. In the meantime, the Kings' marketing arm was busy exploiting the profit potential of the world's greatest hockey player. Wayne was wined and dined, hosted and toasted by the who's who of Tinseltown. He had come a long way from his days selling season tickets in an Indianapolis shopping mall. He was still selling season tickets, but now he clutched

champagne glasses and hob-nobbed with sports minded movie stars and millionaires.

California is a trend-driven city, and if the Kings were to win back McNall's investment, they would have to make hockey the 'in' thing for the smart set. Gretzky gatherings were seeded with a host of well-heeled expatriate Canadians, and these folks brought their famous friends to the parties. David Foster, Alan Thicke, John Candy, Michael J. Fox and Larry Mann were among the most supportive compatriots who celebrated the coming of their famous kin. Hockey became almost *de rigeur* among the Gucci crowd. Season ticket sales rose from less than 5000 subscribers to more than 10,000, and tickets were scooped up for their visits to cities across the National Hockey League. The price of seats in the Great Western Forum nearly doubled overnight, but in the millionaire's market, the cost of a ticket is hardly the buyer's main criterion. If season tickets were a tempting enough commodity for Milton Berle, the Pointer Sisters and Sly Stallone, they became a reasonable business expense for agents and bag-men from Santa Monica to Beverly Hills.

Merchandising the Kings became a huckster's dream; outlets for Kings souvenirs rose from about a dozen locations in greater Los Angeles to more than 200 points-of-sale overnight. Before the season was over, sales of Kings trinkets would more than equal those sold in all previous seasons combined. Prime Ticket, the television broadcaster for the Kings, doubled the number of games they would carry, and hired extra phone workers to help sign up the bevy of new subscribers. The phones at the Kings' ticket office had been ringing off the hook since the ninth of August, and good seats for Gretzky's royal debut were a clear sign of social rank. Hockey investors in the coolest town in America

Left: Gretzky concentrates on the action.

Opposite top: *Mark Messier welcomes Gretzky at his first Edmonton home game in a Kings uniform.*

Opposite bottom: *Gretzky kneels over the Oiler player who got tied up with Gretzky during the action.*

were way out on a limb. Many of the new fans had never seen a hockey game, and those who had followed the fortunes of the Kings were used to comparing their hometown skaters to baseball's lowly Chicago Cubs. Los Angeles is not a city for losers, and this Gretzky kid had better be worth the social investment, or he would very quickly go the way of the hula hoop.

The Great One was indeed great in his first outing in the new-look black and silver jerseys, as the Kings opened their season with an 8-2 routing of the legendary Detroit Red Wings. For the well-schooled hockey fan, a 1-0 game ending in overtime is a night to cherish, but for a room full of neophytes from the fast lane, a big shooting, wide open, 10-goal night was what it would take to bring them back with their friends. Detroit was followed by the future Cup champion Calgary Flames, who were doused 6-5 by the hometown Kings. The New York Islanders and Boston Bruins were similarly crushed on their western tour. Not until the fifth game of the season were the newest fans in hockey sent

home unsatisfied: The Philadelphia Flyers flew into town and left with a 4-1 decision over the Kings. By this time, the fans were sophisticated enough to deal with a loss or two. Many had boned up on the game, and hockey tips and trivia became as valuable at cocktail parties as they were at the rink.

In Los Angeles, King Gretzky had already been accepted as an instant celebrity. Edmontonians, however, are not so used to giving up their most celebrated citizens. Peter Pocklington was still on the hot seat for selling The Great One, and though these fans are more accustomed to the seesaw statistics of the early season, they were not ecstatic about the .500 hockey the Oilers had played in the first six games of the campaign. In Edmonton, and in the mind of Wayne Gretzky, the Big Game would be 99's return to the Northlands Coliseum, on October 19th.

When Gretzky appeared on the ice that night in black and silver, for nearly four minutes Edmonton fans stamped, whistled and cheered a welcome home for their favorite son. The Oilers themselves had a different way of honoring their former captain. His second shift was punctuated by Mark Messier, new captain of the team, and one of the strongest men in professional sports. Messier has a peculiar way of greeting an old friend; he slammed The Great One solidly into the boards, bringing fans to their feet, their loyalties shredded by the desire to both cheer and jeer. The honeymoon was over: it was time to play for keeps.

While Gretzky deked and dazzled his way around the ice, it was to little avail. The defensive capability of his new squad was no match for the Oilers' tenacious and consistent play. Glenn Anderson broke the ice three minutes into the first period, slipping the disk past a shell-shocked Kings goaltender. Marty McSorley, who had come with Gretzky to Los Angeles, tied the affair at the five-minute mark, but that was the closest the Kings would come to winning the match. Gretzky assisted on a Steve Duchesne marker, but try though he might, The Great One was held scoreless in the great western shoot-out. When the final whistle sounded, the hometown Oilers had won the game by a score of 8-6.

Though it is difficult for a major sports star to stay out of the limelight for very long, it was not until several months later that the world would truly stand transfixed by the remarkable skills of the man they call Greatzky. In early February 1989, Gretzky faced Pittsburgh sharpshooter Mario Lemieux in the All-Star Game. Lemieux was bigger, stronger, and younger than Wayne Gretzky, and in the 1989 campaign he was giving The Great One a run for the Art Ross Trophy. This was not the first time Lemieux would face off in an All-Star matchup against Wayne Gretzky, and many felt that this would be Lemieux's year. But for Wayne Gretzky, it was to be a night of magic.

No less than seven of the Campbell team members had played with Wayne Gretzky. He was reunited on his old

home ice with former Oiler teammates Jari Kurri, Mark Messier, Kevin Lowe and Grant Fuhr. Current teammates Luc Robitaille, Steve Duchesne, and Bernie Nicholls represented the hottest sharpshooters in the West. At 1:07 of the first period, the Northlands Coliseum exploded, as Edmonton fans were thrilled by sweet words from another time: '. . . goal by Number 17, Jari Kurri, assist, Number 99, Wayne Gretzky!' Three minutes later the Edmonton devotees erupted once again, as Steve Duchesne fed a loose puck to Gretzky in flight, and 99 delivered the package to goaltender Reg Lemelin right on time, at 4:33. By the half-way mark of the first quarter, goals by Cam Neely and Walt Poddubny had tied the match.

Lemieux and the Wales squad pulled ahead in the second, but they were just not up to the firepower of the West. Three goals by Campbell snipers and some seesaw scoring brought the westerners ahead 6-5 in the third period. A line composed of Kurri, Robitaille and Gretzky is something out of dreamland, but that's exactly what an All-Star team is about, and the line landed a marker halfway through the third period, giving insurance to the Campbell win. At game's end, Gretzky (MVP) and the Campbell team skated into the winner's circle with a 9-5 win.

The ragged edges of Wayne Gretzky's new life were one by one neatly folding into place. His family had expanded by one, with the birth of Paulina Gretzky, and all was right in his world. He had faced his former fans and they had re-ceived him with warmth and forgiveness; his former teammates had been professional. When he returned for the All-Star match, he was the prodigal son. Gretzky had led the Kings into a fight with the Oilers for second place, and had been recognized as a huge success by both fans and financiers. Understandably, Gretzky's scoring numbers had suffered from the move, but he was determined to give Mario Lemieux someone to compete with.

The season came to a close with the Kings in second place in the Smythe Division, and fourth overall in the league. Three Kings, Gretzky, Nicholls and Robitaille, were among the top 10 scorers in the league. Mario Lemieux had finished nearly 30 goals ahead of The Kid, but the Kings had scored 376 goals in the season, more than any other team in the loop. In one season, the Kings had been transformed from a lowly contender for the last spot in the playoffs to a hot ticket with a shot at the big prize.

When the Edmonton Oilers flew into Los Angeles to open their first round series with the Kings, they were on orders to win the matches. There was a lot of pride and ego at stake in the series, and Glen Sather was determined to out-coach the firepower of the Kings. In Game One, the Oilers responded with a 4-3 squeaker over Los Angeles. Game Two saw the Kings battle back and win 5-2 over the visitors. Returning to Edmonton, the Oilers showed Gretzky and the boys a very hard time, shutting them out 4-0, and robbing them in Game Four with last-minute Messier heroics for a 4-3 win.

Opposite: *Gretzky rejoins former teammate Lowe for the NHL's 40th All-Star Game in Edmonton in 1989.*

Top right: *Gretzky with L.A. teammate Luc Robitaille during festivities at the All-Star Game in Edmonton.*

Bottom right: *Gretzky battles his former teammate Jari Kurri during the 1989 Smythe Division semifinals.*

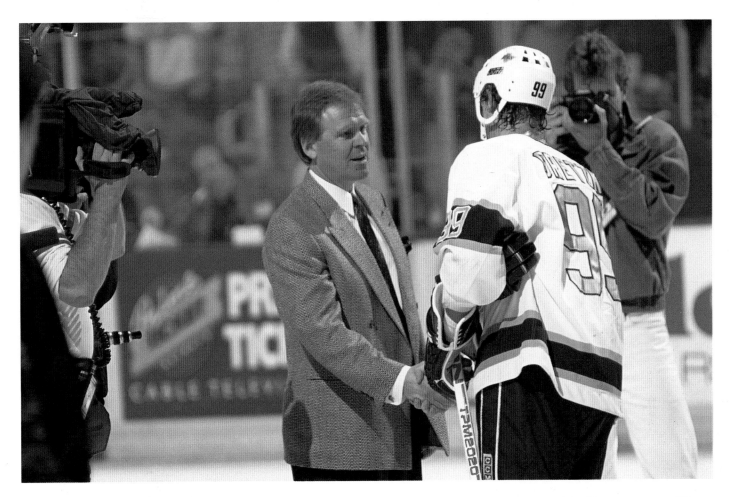

Opposite: *Gretzky in his "office" behind the net.*

Above: *Oilers' coach Glen Sather congratulates Gretzky after the Kings eliminated Edmonton in the 1989 playoffs.*

With the debilitating handicap of a 3-1 series score, the Kings returned to Los Angeles despondent. The odds were very much against them, but the Kings came back flying. They took Game Five in Los Angeles 4-2, and returned to Edmonton to whip the Oilers 4-1. Los Angeles fans were treated to NHL playoff hockey at its best when the teams met for the seventh and deciding game of the Smythe Division semifinals. In the books it may be only a semifinal series, but this was the game of the year for both of these teams. So many had so much riding on this series that it is hard to overstate the fevered excitement of the night.

The game was a seesaw battle, but there was never really any doubt who would win the game. The hockey-mad crowd at the Great Western Forum took it as a given that there would be a happy ending, and The Great One, in Hollywood style, gave them a preview. At the 52-second mark of the first period, he squirted the disk past a confused Grant Fuhr. Though they gave up three, they matched these and scored three unanswered markers, and the crowd went home ecstatic.

It didn't matter that the Kings were swept out of the division finals by the Calgary Flames; they were happy to have finished so far above their accustomed level. Second place in the division was a fine perch from which to launch their next assault on the National Hockey League.

For Wayne Gretzky, there was truly a God in heaven. His scoring had been slowed over the transition – he only potted 54 goals and 114 assists for a points total of 168 – but he was voted the league's Most Valuable Player anyway. There were those who believe that the Hart Trophy for league MVP should have gone to Mario Lemieux for his 199-point season, but keen observers of the game take into account the respective situations of the star centermen. Gretzky, working to build a new unit, had raised his team from 68 points to 91. Lemieux had had a hand-crafted team behind his considerable prowess. The contributions to the game by Gretzky for 1989 clearly outweighed the remarkable 199-point season of the league's highest scorer.

Heading into the 1989-90 season, Gretzky faced his most prestigious challenge to date: to break the all-time points record of the great Gordie Howe. Since Wayne had learned to talk, Gordie Howe had been his idol. The thought of breaking the record of this 26-year veteran was daunting. Gretzky has always understated his triumphs. Overcoming the acknowledged all-time champion of the sport is impossible to understate. This achievement would silence all his detractors.

Gretzky went into the 1989-90 season just 13 points shy of Howe's record. By Game Five The Kid was within striking distance. The target was the Vancouver Canucks, and he needed only four points to equal Howe's record of 1850. He didn't pot one himself in Vancouver, but assisted on three goals, including the game winner. This left him one goal short of a tie, and two short of reaching the pinnacle of his profession. The next game was in Edmonton, Alberta, home of his greatest fans, friends and memories.

Tickets for Game Six on the Great Gretzky Tour were impossible to buy. It was like Stanley Cup weekend in Edmonton. The world press was clamoring for a spot in the press box and companies from Coca-Cola to Xerox were competing for hotel catering facilities in Edmonton's finest inns. Gordie Howe was having the time of his life. His record was

Left: *The Greatest One receives a heartfelt embrace from his father after Wayne surpassed Gordie Howe's career record for points. Walter has served as coach, mentor, guidance counselor and friend to his son from the time Wayne first strapped on the blades to the present day.*

to be eclipsed, but it was to be done by The Kid, Gordie's biggest fan.

Gretzky found a hole early in the game and tied the record. He played nearly every minute, but at the end of two periods, The Great One was still not the greatest one. The 50-minute mark came and went, but still the Oilers held Gretzky. The Kings were down a goal. The score was 4-3 with barely a minute left in the game. The Kings called a time out and regrouped. Steve Duchesne threw the puck across the ice to Dave Taylor and Wayne Gretzky. In the twinkle of an eye, Number 99 hit 1851 and rewrote the record book. Wayne Gretzky was the highest scoring player in the history of the game.

The game ground to a halt as hockey's most illustrious persons came to center ice with gifts and fine words for their most prized asset. Gordie Howe and NHL President John Ziegler, Jr. brought him gold, silver and diamonds. His best friends in the world were in uniform and with him in the triumph they had helped him to achieve.

But the game wasn't over. Wayne Gretzky had broken the all-time scoring record, but there was a game on the line. Only one thing could sweeten the magic of the night: the Kings would win, and Wayne would poke the game winner

himself. Early in the overtime session Gretzky took a pass from John Tonelli and smoked it by Bill Ranford, a storybook ending for the Crown Prince of hockey.

Closing in on season's end, the Kings went into a funk, and management did everything, including trade star sharpshooter Bernie Nicholls, to shake things up. Injuries and roster adjustments kept the Kings from the top end of the Smythe Division, and April found them in fourth place, 24 points behind the division leader. Gretzky was injured toward the end of the season, and the Kings would open the spring season in Calgary, without the help of either Wayne or Larry Robinson, the Hall of Fame defenseman who had joined the Kings at the start of the season.

The Kings were down 3-1 in Game One when they found the wings of champions. Sticks clashed, pucks whirled across the ice, and when the Zamboni rolled out, it was Kings 5, Flames 3. Game Two was dominated by Calgary's Stanley Cup defenders, who sent the Kings home with a 8-5 spanking. Still nursing an ailing shoulder, The Kid signed up for a spot on the lineup card for Game Three in Los Angeles. It was a close game of shifting play and shuffling goaltenders which went into overtime at ones. Tony Granato's fourth-period marker set the series score at 2-1 Kings.

Right: *The Kings swarm off the bench to celebrate with Gretzky after The Great One became The Greatest One, compiling career point number 1851.*

Below: *Wayne Gretzky and Gordie Howe: two gentlemen superstars whose names are synonymous with the game of hockey.*

Tuesday night in Los Angeles saw the Kings in a rout. At the end of three periods, everybody had scored, and the Flames headed home, down three games to one after a 12-4 humiliation.

Calgary pulled within one game of evening up the set in a 5-1 victory on home ice. Game Six was a seesaw battle which saw the Kings down 4-3 in the final minutes of the game. Gretzky fired from the faceoff and hit Steve Duchesne, who blinked the light and tied the game. In double overtime, after the Flames had seen a goal called back, Mike Krushelnyski flicked a loose puck past a startled Mike Vernon and the Kings headed for the division final. The Kings became one of four clubs in history to eliminate the Cup defending team two years running.

The series against Edmonton was disappointing, to say the least. Wayne was injured again, and the Kings were swept by the best team in hockey. Edmonton went on to defeat Chicago in six games and walked over Boston in five to win their fifth Stanley Cup. Wayne's good friend Mark Messier was voted Most Valuable Player in the NHL, and Wayne himself regained his throne, winning the Art Ross Trophy for his 142 points.

The Great One and the Kings finally began to deliver on their promises in the 1990-91 campaign. They had developed an explosive scoring touch coupled with a new, improved defense corps, anchored by Larry Robinson and Steve Duchesne. With Gretzky in the leading role and Tony Granato and Tomas Sandstrom as his supporting cast, they won their first Smythe Division Oscar.

Although the big bombers often get the credit, the Kings couldn't have won their crown without the backstage help of their defensive technicians. Goaltender Kelly Hrudey had his finest season as a professional, while Marty McSorley and Steve Duchesne both had All-Star seasons on the blue-line. McSorley, who was best known for his skills as The Great One's bodyguard, tied for league lead in plus/minus with a rating of +48.

With Gretzky winning his 10th Art Ross Trophy and the Kings assured of home-ice advantage in the early playoff rounds, the fine folks in Tinseltown were making plans for a Lord Stanley love-in. Unfortunately, there would be no curtain calls for the Kings in 1991.

After surviving a scare from the Vancouver Canucks, the Kings prepared to meet the defending champion Edmonton Oilers. The Oilers, who needed an overtime victory in the seventh game to dispose of the Calgary Flames in their first round tilt, were a tired hockey club when they arrived in L.A. for the series. Although the Oilers' bones were aching, their spirit was willing, and they wrote a Hollywood script of their own.

In the Smythe finals, the Kings were battered and bruised by the Edmonton bullies. Craig Muni was a one-man wrecking crew, knocking both Tomas Sandstrom and Rob Blake out of the playbill. The Oilers were a real headache for the Kings, especially for Wayne Gretzky, who suffered a serious ear injury after stepping in front of a slapshot from the point. The Kings couldn't ascend the throne with these key injuries, and dropped the series in six games.

At season's end, Gretzky's old teammate Jari Kurri was sent to the Kings from the Flyers in exchange for Steve Kasper and Steve Duchesne. Although the price was high, Bruce McNall sensed that the addition of Kurri to Gretzky's wing would give the Kings an edge. Gretzky would once again be setting up the man who made him the most helpful player in the history of the game. Hockey fans around the world could look forward to seeing the most productive line the game has ever known, led by The Great One himself, Wayne Gretzky.

Opposite left: *Gretzky receives the Hart Trophy in 1989.*

Opposite right: *Gretzky's the proud father holding his infant daughter, Pauline.*

Opposite below: *At the end of the 1990-91 season, Wayne's old Oiler teammate Jari Kurri was traded to the Kings.*

Right: *Gretzky and the Kings survived a scare from the Vancouver Canucks in the 1991 playoffs.*

CHAPTER 5 GRETZKY'S FIRST AUTOBIOGRAPHY

Wayne Gretzky's first official autobiography is more commonly known as the NHL Record Book. The Great One began his literary career on October 13, 1979, the night he made his debut in the National Hockey League. His opponents that night were the Chicago Blackhawks, 19,000 screaming denizens and a horde of media with their poison pens poised to dismiss the talents of the new kid on the NHL block.

It seems fitting that the first NHL goal scored by the Edmonton Oilers should be set up by the man who would shatter the NHL's all-time assists record and lead the league in helpers every year he has played. At 9:49 of the first period of the Oilers' NHL debut, Kevin Lowe scored the Oilers' first goal, assisted by Drew Callighen and Wayne Gretzky. The Kid didn't get around to scoring one for himself until October 14th, when his goal late in the third period against Glen Hanlon gave the Oilers a tie with the Vancouver Canucks.

Slowly but surely, Gretzky convinced his detractors that he was the genuine article. He entered the record books for the first time on February 15, 1980, when he tied Billy Taylor's 33-year-old single-game assists record by setting up seven goals against the Washington Capitals.

Thanks to some NHL back-room shenanigans, Gretzky

54

Opposite: *Despite the concerted efforts of Bill Barber (7), Gretzky fires the puck into the vacated Flyers' cage to become the first player to score 50 goals in less than 50 games on December 30, 1981.*

Right: *Gretzky in action during his first NHL campaign. The new kid on the block was about to claim his throne.*

Overleaf: *Gretzky fires the puck past Don Edwards for his 77th goal of the 1981-82 season, eclipsing Phil Esposito's 11-year-old single-season mark, on February 24, 1982.*

never received credit for his first scoring record. In 1979-80, he scored 51 goals and assisted on 86 others for a points total of 137, destroying the previous freshman mark of 91 set by Mike Bossy in 1977-78. However, the NHL determined that because Gretzky had played in the WHA, ostensibly another professional league, he wasn't really a rookie. Therefore, he wouldn't be eligible for Rookie of the Year or qualified to set any rookie scoring marks. The public howled, the critics smirked and Gretzky smiled, knowing there would be plenty of opportunities for him to make a lasting impression on the record books.

Gretzky, who actually tied for the scoring lead with Marcel Dionne in 1979-80 but lost the Art Ross Trophy to the L.A. Kings star on goals (Dionne had 53 to Gretzky's 51), captured his first Hart and Lady Byng trophies in 1980. By the time the 1980-81 season rolled around, Gretzky was ready to write his own record book, and set about smashing two records held by two of the game's all-time greats.

Ironically, he set both marks in the same game, against the Colorado Rockies, on April Fool's Day, 1981. On that evening, the joke was on those critics who said Gretzky was too small and too slow to play in the NHL. The Great One picked up two assists to break Bobby Orr's single-season assist mark of 102 and Phil Esposito's single-season points record of 152.

As the 1981-82 campaign was about to begin, Gretzky made an important adjustment to his playing style. He determined that because most defenders played him to pass, he would make a concerted effort to shoot more often. It was a decision that was to make Wayne Gretzky the sports story of the year.

Gretzky started the season by scoring in seven of his first 10 games, and by the time the campaign was 30 games old, he already had 31 goals. Unfortunately for twine tenders around the NHL, The Great One was just getting warmed up. He went on a scoring spree, firing goals in nine straight

Left: *The fans salute the new single-season goal-scoring hero.*

Below: *The Great One wipes a tear from the cheek of Phil Esposito after wiping his name from the NHL Guide and Record Book.*

Opposite: *A trio of MVP's – Richard, Howe and Gretzky – gather around Walter Gretzky at the 1983 NHL Awards ceremony.*

contests, including an unbelievable 14 goals in five games. On December 30, 1981, against the Philadelphia Flyers, Gretzky lit the lamp five times to give him 50 goals in only 39 games, smashing a mark that was thought to be untouchable. Only Maurice 'Rocket' Richard and Mike Bossy had reached the half-century mark in goals in 50 games. Not only had Gretzky turned the trick in less than 40 games, he had also reached the 100-point mark, making 200 points not only attainable but nearly certain.

The next target for Number 99 was Phil Esposito's mark of 76 goals in a season. For Wayne Gretzky in 1981-82, it wasn't a question of if, but merely a matter of when. On February 24, 1982, against Don Edwards and the Buffalo Sabres, Gretzky scored his 77th goal of the year at the 13:34 mark of the third period, erasing Esposito's 11-year-old mark from the record books. On March 25, 1982, Gretzky compiled his 200th point of the season, and when the curtain fell on the schedule, Gretzky had recorded 92 goals and 212 points. Along the way, he still managed to draw 120 assists to break his own single-season mark. The Great One, who was held pointless in only eight games during the 80-date schedule, registered a record 10 hat-tricks, had four games in which he fired four goals or more, and 14 games in which he registered at least five points.

Although there are those who would say that Gretzky slumped the next season, falling to 196 points, he still re-wrote another couple of chapters in the record book. He set up his Oiler teammates 125 times in 1982-83, creating a new assists watermark and marking the first time Number 99 registered more assists than the next leading scorer had points. He also eclipsed Guy Lafleur's consecutive point-scoring streak of 28 games by managing at least one point in 30 consecutive games. More important for Gretzky, however, was the undeniable fact that the Edmonton Oilers were becoming a complete hockey team. They erased the bitter memories of their upset loss to the L.A. Kings in 1982 by advancing to the 1983 Stanley Cup finals. Although the Oilers lost in straight games to the New York Islanders, they had made an important statement: they were more than a one-man show.

In many ways, the 1983-84 season was the greatest of Gretzky's incredible career. He opened the season by picking up at least one point in each of his first 51 games, smashing the mark he had established the season before. In fact, Gretzky caused considerable headaches for the NHL's statistics office with his record-breaking run. When the league first started keeping records of consecutive scoring streaks in the 1970s, they programmed the computer to recognize only two-digit totals. Gretzky, who compiled 153 points in his 51-game reign of excellence, forced the league to update their now-ancient technology.

His amazing run of point prosperity ended on January 28, 1984, when Markus Mattson, a journeyman netminder with the Los Angeles Kings, shut down the scoring machine. It

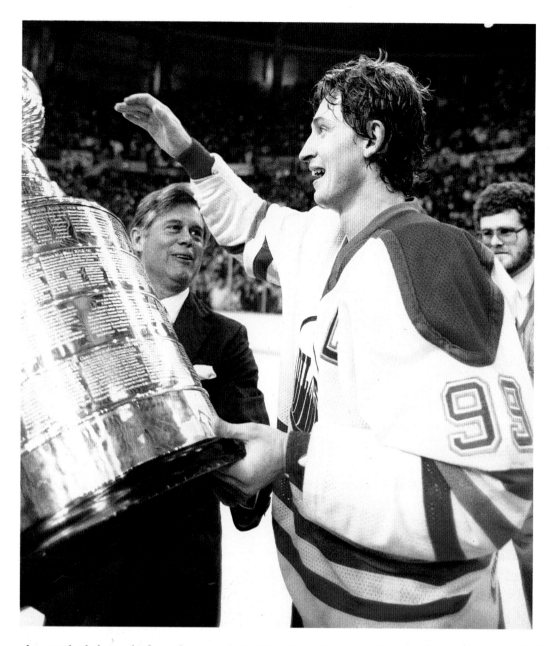

Left: *Despite all the accolades, awards, and All-Star selections, the biggest prize eluded Gretzky's grasp until May 19, 1984. After the Oilers' 5-2 victory over the Islanders in Game Five of the Stanley Cup finals, The Great One finally got the chance to salute Lord Stanley's silver chalice.*

also marked the end of another streak for The Great One. Since his NHL debut in 1979, Gretzky had missed only one NHL game, a match against St. Louis on October 30, 1979. After his points streak ended against the Kings, Gretzky sat out the next six games, nursing an injured shoulder. When he returned to action on February 15, he would only go scoreless in one game through to the end of the season. When the paperwork was done and the results computed, Gretzky had notched his second 200-point campaign, recording 87 goals and 118 assists. He played in 74 games in the 1983-84 season and gathered at least one point in 72 of them. It is doubtful whether anyone will ever be able to match that milestone of consistency.

More important to Gretzky were the team goals that his streak had enabled the Oilers to reach. In only their fifth year in the NHL, the Oilers were the regular season champions, finishing the schedule with a league-leading 119 points and a record-breaking 446 goals. The victory train didn't stop there. The Oilers burned through the post-season, meeting adversaries head-on and summarily depositing them on the playoff scrap heap. The four-time champion N.Y. Islanders, shocked at the defensive blanket the Oilers threw over them in a 1-0 loss in the first game of the 1984 finals, meekly handed over the scepter to the new

kids on the block, surrendering their throne in five games.

Wayne Gretzky and his Edmonton Oiler teammates entered the 1984-85 season as defending Stanley Cup champions, a remarkable achievement for a team that had only been in the NHL for five years. He made slight adjustments to his playing style again in the 1985 campaign, but this time it amounted to leaving the puck in the slot for Jari Kurri, who buried 71 pucks behind enemy netminders in the 1984-85 season. Number 99 gift-wrapped most of Kurri's 71 himself.

Gretzky had his third 200-point campaign in 1984-85, upping his previous total from 205 to 208. Gretzky also led the loop in goals with 73, but it was his play-making that drew accolades from the scribes for most of the year. Gretzky set another single-season assists mark, setting up his teammates 135 times, the same number of points that Jari Kurri compiled in finishing second on the scoring parade. Gretzky attained a personal milestone on December 19, reaching the 1000-point plateau in only his 424th NHL game. As is his custom, Gretzky hit this historic highlight with flair, victimizing the Los Angeles Kings with a six-point evening. All in all, just another year in the office for Number 99.

For Gretzky, however, the real season began with the

Right: *In addition to a plethora of NHL awards, Gretzky also earned more than a few corporate-sponsored accolades. Here he accepts the Emery Edge plus/minus rating from Gordie Howe (**far right**).*

Right: *The Moose is loose. Mark (Moose) Messier and Wayne Gretzky celebrate the Oilers' second straight trip into the Stanley Cup winner's circle, May 30, 1985. Messier fired a pair of unassisted goals and Gretzky had four points in Edmonton's 8-3 victory over Philadelphia in the decisive game.*

Stanley Cup playoffs, and in the 1985 post-season, he re-wrote the post-season chapter of the record book, setting new standards for playoff performers with 17 goals and 30 assists and a new spring season high watermark of 47 points. Of course, Gretzky had set playoff records before, erasing Mike Bossy's standard of 35 post-season points in 1983 with 38 points. However, in 1985, with every contender gunning to upset the defending champion Oilers, Gretzky turned up the heat, notching a new slot for his name among other playoff immortals. In the finals against Philadelphia, with the series tied at one game apiece, Gretzky took matters into his own hands. He fired three first-period goals to give the Oilers the series lead, and Edmonton coasted from there. When the ice was cleared and the champagne had been poured, Wayne Gretzky had another piece of silverware to add to his trophy case: his first Conn Smythe Trophy as the playoff MVP.

As outstanding as his career had been, Gretzky outdid even himself in 1986, fashioning the best statistical season of his career. Although he collected his fewest goals since his freshman campaign, slipping 'only' 52 pucks over opposition goal lines, Gretzky set up a staggering 163 goals, establishing a record that will certainly stand the test of time. Counting his assists alone, he still would have won the scoring title by 22 points. When the 80-game schedule had run its course, Gretzky had compiled 215 points, his fourth 200-point season. The Kid played all 80 games and picked up at least one point in 77 of them, another Herculean effort that may never be equalled. In a season of outstanding achievements, a couple of evenings stand out. On December 11, he set up seven goals against the Chicago Blackhawks, and on Valentine's Day, Gretzky broke the hearts of the Quebec Nordiques by assisting on seven goals again, the third time in his career he rolled a lucky seven.

Edmonton, who ended up first overall in the NHL with 119 points, rolled into the playoffs looking for a third straight Stanley Cup championship. However, as was the case in 1982, Gretzky's individual heroics during the regular season went for naught as the Oilers' well ran dry in a seven-game second round loss to the Calgary Flames.

The Oilers and Gretzky refocused their objectives in 1986-87, concentrating on team defense instead of all-out, firewagon offense. As a result, Gretzy's numbers were down considerably, though he did lead the league in goals (62), assists (121) and points (183), recording more assists than the next leading scorer had points for the second straight season. The highlight of his season came on November 22, 1986, when he became the 13th NHL player to score 500 goals. His victims on this night were the Vancouver Canucks, and again Gretzky accomplished the feat with dramatic flair, firing a hat trick to reach the historic plateau. Surprisingly, there were actually some 'lowlights' to the Gretzky season. For the first time in his career, he didn't record a point in the opening game of the season, and for the first time since he was rookie, he went three games without a point, experiencing his first 'slump' as the season was wearing down and a nagging foot injury was limiting his usual effectiveness.

The Oilers, with Gretzky leading the way, made sure there would be no repeat of the playoff disappointments of the previous year, winning their third Stanley Cup in four years. The Great One led all playoff scorers with 34 points.

In many ways, the 1987-88 campaign was the most satisfying of Gretzky's career, even though it was his worst offensive year since his freshman season. Gretzky fell victim to the injury bug in 1988, missing 13 games with a knee injury and another three with an eye injury. However, when he returned to action, he had his sights on his first all-time career mark. On March 1, in a game against the Los Angeles Kings, he pushed Gordie Howe's name off the top rung of the

NHL's all-time assists list. At the 12:44 mark of the first period, Gretzky slipped a pass to Jari Kurri to register his 1050th NHL assist, becoming the league's career leader in gift-giving.

For Wayne Gretzky, the all-time assists mark is the most satisfying of all his personal achievements. Gretzky has always believed his greatest strength as a hockey player is his ability to anticipate the flow of play a split-second before it happens. He takes more pride in delivering the puck to a teammate than in shooting it, and it took him only 681 games to prove it by placing his name above Gordie Howe's in the NHL bible.

Although he went home without the Art Ross and Hart trophies for the first time since 1981, Gretzky attacked the playoffs with a new passion, and the results were obvious to any opponent who came face to face with the revitalized superstar. He set a new playoff record with 31 assists and led the Oilers to the winner's circle again, returning two valuable pieces of silverware to his collection: the Stanley Cup and the Conn Smythe Trophy.

With a new Cup ring on his finger and another championship banner hanging from the rafters of the Northlands Coliseum, Gretzky sat back to enjoy what should have been his most relaxing summer. However, no one could have predicted that when training camp reopened in September, Wayne Gretzky would be training in Victoria, British Columbia, with the Los Angeles Kings. The NHL records that Gretzky stood poised to topple would have to fall in the City of Angels.

In 1988-89, Wayne Gretzky would have to take a statistical back seat to the marvelous Mario Lemieux, who won his second Art Ross Trophy and tied Gretzky for the league lead in assists. Regardless of Lemieux's dramatics, the story of the year was the coronation of The Great One.

The next record on Gretzky's hit parade was the 600-goal plateau, a mark reached by only four players in NHL history. In a November 23rd game against Detroit, Gretzky racked up five assists and his 600th goal. He also recorded at least one point in his first 31 games as a King before being silenced for the first time on December 17, when the North Stars quieted The Great One's storm.

As the schedule reached its conclusion, considerable attention was being focused on Gretzky's run at the most elusive record of all time: Gordie Howe's career points mark. After being kept off the board in consecutive matches in February, Gretzky racked up 33 points in his last 17 games to fall 13 points shy of the mark. The old cliché 'wait 'til next year' was never so appropriate.

As the 1989-90 season opened, the hockey world looked to the sixth game of the schedule for Gretzky to hit the mark, counting on his career average of 2.3 points per game. The sixth game, as luck would have it, was to be played in Edmonton on October 15, 1989. It may be tempting to believe that The Kid saved his fire for the Oilers, but the numbers show that he was right on time, entering the Northlands just one point short of the mark.

No Hollywood screenwriter could have dreamed up a better script for Gretzky to perform then the masterpiece he delivered in Edmonton on that October evening. Midway through the first period, Gretzky fed a pass to Bernie Nicholls, who buried the puck behind Bill Ranford to tie the record. As the game wore on, Gretzky struggled to escape the blanket that the Oilers' designated pest, Esa Tikkanen, had thrown over him, but was unable to swat the buzzing Finn.

Although he couldn't have planned it the way it ultimately turned out, Gretzky waited until the Kings were trailing

Opposite: *Wayne Gretzky after capturing his fifth consecutive Seagram Award as the Player of the Year, July 30, 1986.*

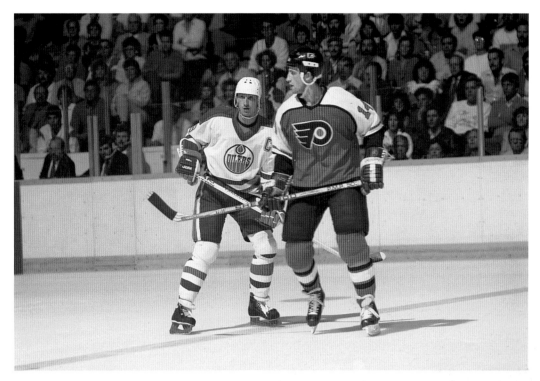

Right: *The Flyers' Ron Sutter keeps a close tab on Gretzky during the 1987 Cup finals.*

Below: *This magic moment. Gretzky celebrates career-point 1851, breaking Gordie Howe's all-time mark, October 15, 1989.*

Above: *Teammates Larry Robinson (19) and Dave Taylor offer Gretzky a hand with a painting by renowned artist LeRoy Neiman commemorating his career-points record.*

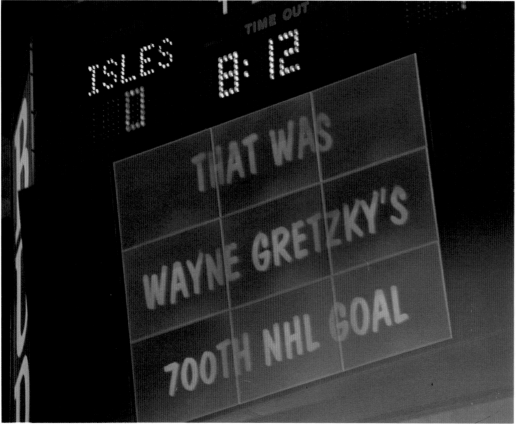

Left: *Every picture tells a story. Gretzky has just become the fourth player in NHL history to score 700 goals in his career.*

Right: *In a move marked by controversy, the city of Edmonton commissioned a statue of Gretzky to be erected outside the Northlands Coliseum. The Oilers' brass, however, were less than anxious to participate in the ceremony, and declined to be involved. Thousands of Gretzky fans felt otherwise, and showered their favorite son with well-deserved admiration.*

4-3 with goaltender Mario Gosselin on the bench for an extra attacker to paint the final stroke on his masterpiece. Gretzky broke free in front of the Oilers' net, accepted a clever pass that hopped off Dave Taylor's stick, and swiftly fired a backhand over Ranford's shoulder into the top shelf. The Great One was now the Greatest.

There were still a few plateaus for Gretzky to climb, and still a couple of accolades to receive. Off the ice, he was named the Associated Press Athlete of the Decade, the first hockey player to be so honored. On the pond, he scored his 700th NHL goal on January 3, 1991, in a 6-3 win over the New York Islanders. When he became the first NHL player to hit the 2000-point mark on October 26, 1990, against Winnipeg, mathematicians worked overtime calculating when he would most likely register his 3000th point.

At last count, Wayne Gretzky has established 55 regular-season, playoff, All-Star and career records. In fact, there are only a few offensive records that Gretzky is yet to break, including Darryl Sittler's mark of 10 points in a single game and Gordie Howe's count of 801 career goals. The only other marks left for Number 99 to conquer are records that concern longevity. Even with his athletic prowess, it's doubtful that he will surpass Gordie Howe's 32 years in professional hockey, but don't close the book on that chapter yet.

CHAPTER 6 SUMMER HOCKEY: THE INTERNATIONAL STORY

One of the most intriguing aspects of Wayne Gretzky's marvelous career has been the unselfish way he has raised the game to new heights. In this era of the multi-year, multi-million dollar contracts, athletes like Gretzky, who play their sport with a dedication to 'we' instead of 'me,' are rare. Nowhere is this more evident than in Gretzky's international appearances, where he has always represented his country with pride and dignity. Gretzky has never refused the opportunity to wear the Red Maple Leaf.

Wayne Gretzky has been the leading scorer in every international tournament in which he has participated. Despite the mental fatigue of an 80-game season, the aching bones following lengthy playoffs and the bruised ego of early post-season exits, not only has Gretzky been ready to pull on the jersey, he has also always given his all.

His first taste of international success came in the 1978 World Junior Hockey Championships. Canada, having only recently returned to international hockey competition, chose a group of Canadian junior players to represent the country at the 1978 tournament in Montreal, Quebec. Gretzky, who at 16 years old had risen to the top of the

Ontario Hockey Association star lineup with the Sault Ste. Marie Greyhounds, was one of 10 OHA players to earn a berth on the team. Canada wasn't given much of a chance to win the affair, but with a squad stacked with such future NHL stars as Rob Ramage, Mike Hartsburg, Bobby Smith, Mike Gartner and Brad Marsh, the young group of Canucks weren't about to let the critical opinion of a few overzealous scribes ruin their first run at the stars from the USSR and Czechoslovakia.

Canada breezed through the preliminary round with a perfect 3-0 record, with Gretzky leading the way firing hat tricks against the Czechs and the West Germans. The medal round, however, was a far more difficult task. For the first time in his young career, Gretzky was outclassed. Canada lost a close 4-3 decision to the Soviets, but bounced back to defeat Sweden 6-5. Against the Czechs, a team they had handled easily in the earlier round, they fell apart, unable to protect a lead in the third period and losing 6-5. Although Gretzky was held to only four points in the three-game medal round, he still won the scoring title with 17 points, fashioned on eight goals and nine assists. Canada had to

Left: *A youthful Wayne Gretzky after the Team Canada Juniors fell to the Soviet Junior squad 4-3 in the 1978 World Junior Championships, December 28, 1977.*

settle for the bronze medal, a door-prize that sat uneasily with Gretzky and his mates. Future international matches would prove that Canada could match the hockey talent found on any sheet of ice in the world, but in 1978, the 16-year-old phenomenon and his inexperienced teammates still had a lot to learn.

By 1981, when the second Canada Cup tournament was held, many of the juniors who succumbed to the Soviets in the 1978 tournament were in the NHL, and were vying for posts on the Team Canada roster. The Soviet Union, who had destroyed a group of NHL All-Stars in the 1979 Challenge Cup showdown, were heavy favorites to unseat Canada and win their first Canada Cup trophy.

Gretzky had already established himself as the newest NHL star, winning his first scoring title in 1980-81. Now, for the first time, fans around the world were going to witness The Kid at his best, playing alongside the most gifted players in the world: Lafleur, Bossy, Bryan Trottier, Denis Potvin, Perreault, Viacheslav Fetisov, Stastny and Vladimir Krutov. However, the Canada Cup tournament was to be a bitter pill for The Great One to choke down.

Canada, led by Gretzky and Bossy, sailed through the preliminary rounds, with a tie against Czechoslovakia the only blemish on their record. In the final game before the medal round, the Canadians blasted the USSR 7-3, and although Gretzky didn't play an overpowering role in the victory, he was a key component in the win.

The tables turned quickly when the money was on the line. The Soviets were master technicians, and knew exactly when to use maximum effort. The Canadian team, torn apart by internal strife, was easy prey for the swarming Russians in the one-game Canada Cup final. The USSR, echoing its performance in the 1979 Challenge Cup, dominated from the opening draw. When the ice was cleared, the score was Soviets 8, Canada 1.

The reaction of Canadians from Victoria to Gander was swift and harsh. They needed a scapegoat, and they settled on The Kid, who, in their minds, could score bundles in the meaningless games, but had folded up like a cheap suitcase when the pressure was on. Even the tournament organizers seemed to take this approach. Gretzky led all scorers in the tournament with five goals and seven assists, yet he failed to win an MVP vote and was neglected in the All-Star team balloting. Gretzky went into seclusion for five days following the disaster, and while resting and analyzing this most

Top: *Although he was only 16 years old, Wayne Gretzky won the World Junior Championships scoring title.*

Right: *The soon-to-be Great One was humbled by the tough international competition, an event that only served to toughen his resolve.*

embarrassing of defeats, he prepared himself for the upcoming NHL season, conditioning himself against the adverse fan reaction. He answered his critics, and his own doubts, by having perhaps the greatest season in the history of professional sports.

The next Canada Cup tournament was not scheduled until 1984, and with the Oilers beginning to gel as an NHL powerhouse, it seemed doubtful that an appearance in the World Hockey Championships would be possible. After all, the team that represents Canada at the World Championships is made up of NHL players whose teams either missed the playoffs or were eliminated in the first round, and Gretzky expected to be playing NHL hockey until late May. However, despite the incredible season Gretzky manufactured in the 1981-82 season, the Oilers fell victim to the playoff jinx and made an early, unexpected exit in the spring season.

The Oilers' lapse in the 1982 playoffs may have been one of the biggest upsets in NHL history, but Wayne Gretzky didn't have time to reflect on his team's early post-season demise. Almost immediately, he accepted an offer to join Team Canada in Helsinki, Finland.

For Wayne Gretzky, there was only one way to avenge what had become a lost season. After giving up his summer to participate in the Canada Cup, rewriting the NHL record book with 92 goals and 212 points in the regular season and suffering an embarrassing defeat in the playoffs, no one could have expected Gretzky, who was so reluctant to travel by air, to jump on a plane for a 12-hour flight and lace on the blades for Canada in what was commonly seen as a losing cause.

Canada had not won the world hockey title since 1961, and the rag-tag group of players assembled to represent the country at the world tourney was seldom the best talent available. It is a fitting tribute to the way Wayne Gretzky

views his place in sport and his role as an athletic ambassador for Canada that, not only did he answer the bell, but he also very nearly achieved what many experts felt was an impossible goal – winning a gold medal for Canada.

The Canadian team, composed of a host of NHL greats including Gretzky, Bill Barber, Darryl Sittler, Bob Gainey, Dale Hawerchuk and Gilles Meloche, came out blazing, marking six goals in the first 10 minutes of their game against Finland on the way to an easy 9-2 romp. After a disheartening loss to Czechoslovakia, in which the Czechs counted three goals in the final four minutes, the Canuck squad rebounded to tie Sweden and down West Germany before losing a close 4-3 decision to the USSR. Led by Gretzky, the Canadians moved into the medal round with a real chance at the gold. Forced to play Russia on consecutive days, Gretzky and his troops were confident they could match the Soviets' firepower. However, the Canucks couldn't penetrate the stubborn Soviet defense, and the USSR jumped out to a quick 4-1 lead after only 25 minutes. Undaunted, the Canadians surged back, tying the encounter 4-4 before losing their grip and falling 6-4 to the powerful Soviet squad.

Gretzky was the media darling of the affair, and the target of Soviet shadows. It is a testimony to his endurance that he performed at his accustomed level throughout all the hyperbole and Soviet attention.

The Canadians captured their final two matches, avenging an earlier loss to the Czechs with a convincing 4-2 victory, and sewing all the loose pieces together to destroy Sweden 6-0 in their final contest.

Gretzky, perhaps relieved that his long season was coming to a close, was flying against the Swedes, notching a hat trick and setting up two others for a five-point explosion. Although the gold medal was out of the question, Canada still had a decent shot at the silver if the USSR could defeat

Opposite: *Gretzky is stopped by Soviet netminder Aleksandr Tvzhnykh in the 1978 Junior tournament.*

Top right: *Vladislav Tretiak stymied Team Canada as the USSR captured the 1981 Canada Cup.*

Below: *Tretiak and Gretzky, superheroes of hockey's superpowers.*

the Czechs. The crafty Soviets, however, played just well enough to gain a 0-0 tie with the Czechs, denying Canada the silver medal and taking great joy in doing so. Gretzky had turned in another fine effort, leading all tournament scorers with six goals and eight assists, totals that earned him a spot on the World Tournament All-Star Team.

The Great One's greatest individual season was over. It had started in August with the Team Canada training camp and had ended 10 months later in Finland, after 100 games of top-notch competition. Although it was his finest hour as a hockey player, Gretzky could not savor the moment. Despite his efforts, he had come up empty where it counted – in the winner's circle. He summed it up best, when reminded of the incredible run of success he had achieved throughout the hockey year, by saying, 'It doesn't matter, if you don't win.' Although he couldn't have known it at the time, Wayne Gretzky would never have to wince at the taste of defeat in international play again. There was a world of difference in the mental make-up of Wayne Gretzky when he started his training for the Canada Cup tournament of 1984. The Oilers were Stanley Cup champions, and he had finally tasted the sweet wine of victory. Canada had assembled another top-shelf squad of hockey talent, led by The Great One himself and complemented by Paul Coffey, Michel Goulet, Mike Bossy and John Tonelli.

Despite, or perhaps because of, the great assembly of talent, the Canadian squad was slow to mature, dragging itself through the tournament with two wins, a pair of losses and a tie. On September 10, in the much-awaited rematch with the Soviets, the Canadians gave a flat, almost uninterested performance, losing by a 6-3 score that actually flattered them. As a result of this loss, they would be forced to meet the undefeated Soviet squad two days later in the one-game semifinal. This time, however, the results would be different.

In one of the most exciting games ever, the Canadians battled the USSR team shot-for-shot, goal-for-goal for two periods. In the third, down by a single marker, Gretzky set up the tying goal to force the first overtime match of the tournament. Team Canada had a distinct advantage – the Soviets had never played in a sudden-death extra frame before – and attacked the Soviets full bore. The strategy almost backfired when Vladimir Kovin and Mikhail Varakov sped into the Team Canada zone, two-on-one, with only Paul Coffey back. Coffey intercepted a cross-ice pass, and quickly turned the play back up ice. He threw a pass into the corner, where John Tonelli was waiting. Tonelli fired the

Opposite: *Vladislav Tretiak faces the Quebec Nordiques' Marian Stastny during an NHL-USSR exhibition series held during the 1982-83 season. Tretiak – who shut out the Nordiques 3-0 in this December 30, 1982, tilt – became Gretzky's close ally, sharing a competitive common bond of respect and admiration.*

Right: *Led by Wayne Gretzky, Team Canada returned to the top rung of the international ladder by bringing home the 1984 Canada Cup.*

puck to the point, where Coffey had miraculously re-appeared, and his blueline blast was tipped out of the air by Mike Bossy at the 12:29 mark of overtime.

The victory catapulted Canada into the best-of-three final against Sweden, which was over quickly and painlessly, although the Canucks nearly blew a five-goal lead in the second match before holding on to win 6-5. Wayne Gretzky took particular pride in striding to center ice and holding the Canada Cup trophy high over his head while the masses at the Northlands Coliseum in Edmonton reveled in a boisterous victory salute.

Once again, Gretzky was the tournament's leading scorer,

racking up 12 points in eight games. An All-Star Team selection made the affair even sweeter, but Gretzky took special pride in seeing John Tonelli, a lunch-bucket forward whose work in the corners and constant fore-checking set the table for The Great One's heroics, earn the nod as the tournament MVP. The Great One had followed up his trip to the Stanley Cup penthouse with an emotional ride into the Canada Cup winner's circle.

The next piece of business on the Gretzky agenda, besides helping add another championship banner to the rafters of Northlands Coliseum and blasting holes in the NHL Record Book, was Rendez-Vous '87, an All-Star confrontation between the USSR and the NHL that took place in Quebec City on February 11 and 13, 1987. This meeting was of special interest to Gretzky because his good friend, former Soviet stand-out Vladislav Tretiak, was to be one of the guests of honor at the All-Star gala. Indeed, Gretzky always felt the 1984 Canada Cup win to be something of a letdown because it was accomplished by defeating a Soviet squad that was without the thorn-in-the-side Tretiak, who always saved his best play for the Canadians.

Tretiak, the USSR's greatest goaltender and the first Soviet-trained player to be inducted into the Hockey Hall of Fame, was the key ingredient in the Soviet victories in the 1979 Challenge Cup and the 1981 Canada Cup. The pair formed a mutual admiration society that culminated in Gretzky spending two weeks in Moscow as a guest of the Tretiak family. The first North American television commercial to feature a Soviet athlete paired Gretzky and Tretiak, a humorous, well-written advertisement that gave everyone a good look at the two first men of ice hockey. Gretzky was one of the few North American sportsmen who took time to understand the complexities of the Soviet system and their athletes, and he regards it as one of the great learning experiences of his life.

The Rendez-Vous tournament was a two-game affair that featured a classic Canadian comeback in the first tilt and a methodical Soviet victory in the rubber match. Gretzky, who assisted on all three NHL goals in the second game, led all scorers with four points. All in all, with the lessening of political tensions in the USSR, the event was a fun-filled affair without the behind-the-scenes dramas which had formerly characterized meetings between these two hockey super-powers. It also served as a tasty appetizer for the main course: the 1987 Canada Cup series.

The 1986-87 campaign was a tiring one for Gretzky. The Oilers had to survive a seven-game series against the Philadelphia Flyers before returning to the top of the NHL heap, and for the first time in his career, Wayne Gretzky was tired of hockey. When the invitations went out for the 1987 Canada Cup, he seriously considered returning his with a 'thanks, but no thanks' reply. Thankfully for hockey fans everywhere, Wayne's greatest coach, his dad, stepped in and convinced The Kid to attend. Walter Gretzky used simple logic to change his son's mind: if Wayne didn't participate, he'd be ridiculed by the press and the fans, and if he went and played poorly, he'd be ashamed. There was only one answer: suit up for Team Canada and play the best hockey of his life.

The 1987 Canada Cup stands alone as the most exciting hockey event of the decade. A convention of future Hall-of-Famers was gathered to represent Canada, including Grant Fuhr, Dale Hawerchuk, Mario Lemieux, Mark Messier and Ray Bourque. For the organizers and the fans, everything fell into place. The finals featured the Soviets and Team Canada, with both squads at the top of their game. The anticipation of seeing Wayne Gretzky and Mario Lemieux paired off against the Soviets left the spectators breathless.

After sneaking past the Czechs in the semifinals, helped in part by a couple of serves by Gretzky onto the sticks of Michel Goulet and Mario Lemieux, the finals were set, with Team Canada versus Team USSR in a best-of-three battle.

The three-game set produced high-quality entertainment that hadn't been witnessed on the ice since the infamous Series of the Century in 1972. Each game was decided by

Below: *The opening face-off of Rendez-Vous '87 (l-r:Gretzky, Tretiak, Howe, Beliveau and Fetisov).*

Right: *Gretzky during the All-Star exhibition series at Rendez-Vous '87.*

Left: *The two catalysts in the 1987 Canada Cup victory for Team Canada: Mario Lemieux and Wayne Gretzky.*

Below: *Gretzky tries to shoot but the puck is tipped away during the 1987 Canada Cup.*

Right: *The victors take the spoils: Gretzky with Mario Lemieux during the 1987 Canada Cup.*

identical 6-5 scores, two of them needing extra time to decide. After falling behind 4-1 in Game One, Canada stormed back to take a 5-4 lead, with The Great One scoring the go-ahead marker. The Soviets ruined Gretzky's best-laid plans by tying the affair seconds later, then winning it in overtime. Game Two featured a five-assist effort from Gretzky, including the decisive marker at 10:07 in double overtime. The winning marker, a fluke assisted by the puck fairy, came when Gretzky, parked on the Soviet doorstep, flubbed an easy empty-net shot. The puck dribbled off the blade of his stick and rolled across the crease to Mario Lemieux, who fired the pill into the yawning cage to even the set at one apiece.

The third game was not an affair for the weak of heart. In one hour of intense rivalry and sheer electric excitement, Canada bounced back from 3-0 and 4-2 deficits. The lead changed hands three times before Canada, trapped in an on-ice déjà-vu, scored with 86 seconds left to put the champagne on ice. Just as it would happen in a fairy tale, the series-deciding goal was orchestrated by the prince of hockey, who conducted a three-on-one break with Mario Lemieux and Larry Murphy. Using Murphy as a decoy, Gretzky calmly held on to the puck before feathering it to Lemieux. The Magnificent Mario, the heir apparent to the

Gretzky throne, one-timed a drive to the top shelf and history was made. After the final ticks of the clock, the score stood at 6-5 in Canada's favor.

Gretzky compiled 21 points in only nine games, the highest total he has registered on the international scene. He was named to the tournament All-Star Team and walked away with his second Canada Cup crown, cementing his position as one of sport's all-time clutch performers.

Much has changed since that monumental meeting. The ice hockey cold war is over. The Soviet Union allows its players to cross the ocean and play in the NHL, easing the bitter feud that has existed between the two countries.

The 1991 Canada Cup provided Wayne Gretzky with the opportunity to play for his country for the first time since the trade to Los Angeles. Gretzky led all scorers with 12 points and virtually defeated the United States and Sweden single-handedly as Canada went unbeaten in the pre-season classic and won their fourth Canada Cup title.

Clearly, Gretzky was the star of the show, although he was grounded for the second game of the finals after taking a bruising hit from U.S. blueliner Gary Suter in Game One. Team Canada may have painted the finishing touches without the Great One, but the 1991 Canada Cup remained Gretzky's masterpiece.

CHAPTER 7 THE GRETZKY EMPIRE

Gretzky may be recognized as the greatest hockey player ever, but his achievements are not restricted to the rink. He is also well-known as a philanthropist and businessman. In recent years his business skills have been bolstered by his friend and boss, Bruce McNall, who knows a thing or three about turning money into more money.

While in Edmonton, Gretzky invested in a blind pool known as Ventana Equities Inc. A blind pool is a bit like a poker game. The money is invested in long shot deals, and those holding stakes either lose all or win big. In the case of Ventana, they did pretty well. Gretzky's name brought money from people who would never have risked their savings otherwise, and the sensible management of Ian Barrigan brought returns to shareholders. Barrigan, Gretzky's personal business manager at the time, took Wayne through the paces while negotiating endorsement contracts with Nike, Nissan, General Mills, Gillette, American Express and Titan. This was not Wayne's first exposure to big business – after all, he did write his own contract with Nelson Skalbania back in the Indianapolis Racer days – but now he was learning the ropes of business outside of ice hockey.

By the time he arrived in Los Angeles, he was in fairly good shape to handle his growing fortune. While his business is professionally managed by his long-time agent Gus Badali, The Kid keeps his hand in. He invests in bricks and mortar, but he is also not afraid to put some cash into things that he loves.

Gretzky's first purchase of a sports franchise was in 1985, when he bought a piece of the Ontario Hockey League's Belleville Bulls. Later, he bought the Hull Olympics of the Quebec Major Junior Hockey League. The Great One has not restricted his sporting investments to hockey, however, and in 1991 he was part of a group that purchased the Toronto Argos football club from Harry Ornest, another expatriate Canadian in Los Angeles. In 1989, the Canadian Football League team had been granted rights to hold their games in Toronto's new and very impressive Skydome. The new Argos partnership of Gretzky, McNall and comedian John Candy intend to turn a deficit operation around by filling up the huge multi-use facility with football fans. The first plank in their business platform was to bring Raghib 'Rocket' Ismail, the most explosive and sought-after college ball player in the world, into the fold. The Rocket's $26 million price tag may well have been more than the entire

Left: *Gretzky's new business partners, Bruce McNall and Hollywood funnyman John Candy, purchased the Canadian Football League's Toronto Argos.*

Right: *Gretzky and McNall sign Heisman Trophy winner Raghib 'Rocket' Ismail to ply his trade for the Toronto Argos in the CFL.*

Below: *Golden Pheasant, co-owned by Gretzky and McNall, wins the 10th running of the Arlington Million, crowning Gretzky's place in the sport of kings.*

Left: *Charity sports events, from the links to the tennis courts, have always been an off-ice priority for Gretzky.*

Opposite: *Gretzky with Lisa Howard at the annual Wayne Gretzky Celebrity Sports Classic. Teams of celebrities play baseball to raise money for the Canadian National Institute for the Blind.*

Canadian Football League was worth, but the entrepreneurial trio have set out to change radically the lagging fortunes of the struggling football loop.

Recently, Gretzky has become involved in horse racing through Bruce McNall, whose Summa Stables has owned over 2000 horses, and currently owns around 300 thoroughbreds. It would figure that Gretzky's first horse would follow in his own footsteps; Golden Pheasant's debut took Europe by storm in 1989, upsetting top-ranked Nashwan at Longchamps. In his first 11 starts, Golden Pheasant has won five times, finished second in three, and taken third once.

Through his association with McNall and the major league sporting set, Gretzky has become a part of major inter-sport marketing and investments. In the near future, he will be seen in a cartoon series with Bo Jackson and Michael Jordan. The baseball card collector's market became front page news when McNall and Gretzky purchased a 1910 Honus Wagner card for $425,000. McNall has made a fortune buying rare collectibles, and this purchase may well bring some additional retirement security for both of them.

Gretzky's business investments are an interesting sidebar, but they don't really reveal much about who this man is and what place he holds in the sports world. His endorsement practices, however, indicate the magnitude of his success as a celebrity, and reveal something about the man.

Endorsing products from razor blades to panty hose has become a big part of the sport celebrity scene. Many athletes make more money smiling and pointing at products than they do shooting, dunking or completing passes, and endorsement rights have become hard bargaining points in many major league contracts. Gretzky has been lending his name to Madison Avenue since his emergence as a bright light on the horizon, and he has maintained a rigorous set of standards throughout his career.

Michael Barnett of CorpSport International manages the 'Gretzky Image.' The Gretzky image is that of a handsome, clean living superstar without so much as a hint of scandal or blemish. Each summer he hosts a celebrity fundraiser in his hometown of Brantford, where hockey players rub elbows with the elite of the entertainment world to play tennis or baseball for the benefit of the blind. This kind of stuff is worth solid gold in the agency trade.

Gretzky is the consummate professional on and off the ice. On the ice he has surpassed the wildest dreams of even the most imaginative hockey fan, while in the financial pages he is a veritable case study in marketing success. Wayne Gretzky has lived most of his life in the fast lane, but he's never even had a ticket; he is polite to the press, indulgent with his fans, gives generously to social causes, and voices no political opinions. His display of virtue and clean living ranks The Great One among the most remarkable entertainment professionals of this, or any other time.

INDEX

Numerals in *italics* indicate illustrations

All-Stars, 19, 20, 21, 47, 67, 69, 71, 74
American Press Athlete of the Year Award, 22
Anderson, Glenn, 21, 25, 26, 45
AP Athlete of the Decade, 65
Art Ross Trophy, 20, 24, 27, 31, 45, 53, 55, 62
Avco Cup, 19

Badali, Gus, 18, 76
Bantam League, 14, 15
Barber, Bill, *54*, 68
Barnett, Michael, 78
Barrigan, Ian, 76
Beliveau, Jean, *72*
Belleville Bulls, 76
Birmingham Bulls, 18
Blake, Rob, 53
Bossy, Mike, 55, 59, 61, 67, 69, 71
Boston Bruins, 32, *32*, 44
Bourque, Ray, 72
Brantford, Ontario, 8, 12, 13, 78
Brantford Atom League, 13
Buffalo Sabres, 59

Calgary Flames, 25, 26, 30, 31, 32, 44, 49, 50, 53, 62
Callighen, Drew, 54
Campbell Conference, 45, 46
Canada Cup, 9, 31, 66-70, 71, *71*, 72-74, *74*
Canadian Football League, 76, 78
Candy, John, 43, 76, 77
Carpenter, Bobby, 42
Carson, Jimmy, 38
Challenge Cup, 67, 72
Chicago Blackhawks, 25, 30, 54, 61
Coffey, Paul, *22, 24*, 25, 27, 30, 42, 69, 71
Conn Smythe Trophy, 27, 30, 32, 61, 62
CorpSport International, 78

Detroit Red Wings, 44, 62
Dineen, Bill, 18
Dionne, Marcel, 20, 24, 55
Driscoll, Peter, 19
Duchesne, Steve, 42, 45, 46, 50, 53

Edmonton Oilers, 8, 19, 21, 22, 24, 25, 27, 30, 31, 32, *32*, 38, 40, 42, 44, 45, 46, 49, 50, 53, 54, 59, 60, 61, 62, 65, 68, 69
Edwards, Don, *56-57*, 59
Esposito, Phil, *55*, 55, *58*, 59

Fetisov, Viacheslav, 67, *72*
Fischler, Stan, 20

Foster, David, 43
Fox, Jimmy, 24
Fox, Michael J., 43
Fuhr, Grant, 27, 31, 46, 49, 72

Gadsby, Bill, 26-27
Gainey, Bob, 68
Gartnere, Mike, 66
Gelinas, Martin, 38
Geruliatis, Vitas, 34
Gilbert, Rod, 27
Golden Pheasant, *77*
Gosselin, Mario, 65
Goulet, Michel, 69, 72
Granato, Tony, 50, 53
Gretzky, Brent, *30*
Gretzky, Phyllis, 12, 14, *17*
Gretzky, Pauline 46, *52*
Gretzky, Tony & Mary, 12
Gretzky, Walter, *12*, 12, 13, 14, 15, *17*, *59*, 72

Hanlon, Glen, 54
Hartford Whalers, 20
Hartsburg, Mike, 66
Hart Trophy, 20, 21, 49, *52*, 55, 62
Hatchborn, Len, 14
Hawerchuk, Dale, 68, 72
Hockey Hall of Fame, 50, 72
Houston Aeros, 18
Howard, Lisa, *79*
Howe, Gordie, 15, *15*, 16, 19, 20, *21*, 49, 50, *51*, 55, *59*, *61*, 62, 65, *72*
Howell, Harry, 27
Hrudey, Kelly, 53
Hull Olympics, 76

Indianapolis Racers, 8, 9, 18, *19*, 19, 76
International matches, 66-74
Ishmail, Raghib 'Rocket', 38, 76, *77*

Jackson, Bo, 78
Jones, Janet, 34, *34*, 36, 38, 39, 40, *40*
Jordan, Michael, 78
Junior A Hockey League, 15

Kasper, Steve, 53
Kovin, Vladimir, 69
Krushelnyski, Mike, 38, 53
Krutov, Vladimir, 67
Kurri, Jari, 21, *22*, 25, 26, *26*, 27, 31, *32*, 46, *52*, 53, 60, 62

Lady Byng Trophy, 21, 55
Lafleur, Guy, 59, 67
Lemelin, Reg, *32*, 46
Lemieux, Mario 'The Magnificent', *31*, 31, 45, 46, 49, 62, 72, 74, *74*, *75*
Los Angeles Kings, 14, 20, 24, 36, 38, 39, 42, 43, 44-53, *51*, *53*, 55, 59, 62, 65
Los Angeles Lakers, 34
Lowe, Kevin, 21, 46, 54

McClelland, Kevin, 26
McNall, Bruce, 36, *36*, 38, *39*, 43, 53, 76, *76*
McSorley, Marty, 38, 42, 45, 53

Mann, Larry, 43
Marsh, Brad, 66
Mattson, Markus, 59
Meloche, Gilles, 68
Messier, Mark, 21, *22*, 25, 27, 31, *45*, 45, 46, 53, *61*, 72
Millen, Greg, 14
Minnesota North Stars, 26, 62
Mio, Eddie, *19*, 19
Montreal Canadiens, 21
Moss, Vicki, 34
Most Gentlemanly Player Award, 16
Murphy, Larry, 74
MVP Award, 14, 30, 49, 53, 61, 67, 71

Nadrofsky Steelers, 14
Neely, Cam, 46
Neiman, LeRoy, 64
New England, *see* Hartford Whalers
New York Islanders, 22, *25*, 25, 26, 44, 59, 60
Nicholls, Bernie, 42, 46, 50, 62
Nuni, Craig, 53

Ontario Hockey Association, 15, 66, 76
Ornest, Harry, 76
Orr, Bobby, 20, 21, 55
Oshawa Generals, 16

Park, Brad, 27
Perreault, Gilbert, 67
Peterborough Petes, 15
Philadelphia Flyers, 14, 21, 30, *31*, 31, 44, *54*, 59, 61, 72
Pittsburgh Penguins, 45
Player of the Year, 1986, *62*
Pocklington, Peter, 19, 36, *36*, 37, 38, 39, 40, 44
Poddubny, Walt, 46
Potvin, Denis, 67

Quebec Major Junior Hockey League, 76
Quebec Nordiques, 19, 61, 71

Ramage, Rob, 66
Ranford, Bill, 62, 65
Ranford, John, 50
Rendez-Vous '87, 71-72, 73
Richard, Maurice 'Rocket', *59*, 59
Robinson, Larry, 50, 53, *64*
Robinson, Wayne, 50
Robitaille, Luc, 42, 46, *47*
Rookie of the Year Award, 8, 14, 16, 19, 42, 55

St. Louis Blues, 60
Sandstrom, Tomas, 53
Sather, Glen, 26, 46, *49*
Sault Sainte Marie Greyhounds, 15, 16, 66
Seagram Award, *62*
Sittler, Darryl, 65, 68
Skalbania, Nelson, *18*, 18, 19, 37, 76
Smith, Battlin' Billy, *25*, 25
Smith, Bobby, 16, 66

Smith, Steve, 31
Smythe Division, 21, 24, 27, 30, 31, 46, 49, 50, 53
Sports Illustrated Sportsman of the Year Award, *23*
Stanley Cup, 8, 9, 22, 25, 26, 27, 30, 31, 32, 37, 39, 50, 53, 59, 60, 61, 62, 69, 71
Stastny, Peter, 67, *70*
Sutter, Ron, *63*

Taylor, Billy, 54
Taylor, Dave, 24, 42, 50
Team Canada, 67-74; Juniors, *66*
Team USSR, 72, 74
Thicke, Alan 34, 43
Tikkanen, Esa, *32*, 62
Tonelli, John, 50, 69, 71
Toronto Argonauts, 39, 76
Toronto Young Nationals, 14
Tretiak, Vladislav, *69, 70*, 72, *72*
Trottier, Bryan, 67
Tvzhnykh, Aleksandr, *68*

Vachon, Rogie, 43
Vancouver Canucks, 30, 37, 49, *53*, 53, 54, 62, 65
Varakov, Mikhail, 69
Ventana Equities, Inc., 76
Vernon, Mike, 32, 53

Wales Division, 46
Washington Capitals, 54
Watters, Tim, 42
Wells, Jay, 42
Whitlow, Cliff, *8*
Winnipeg Jets, 19, 26, 30, 31, 65
World Hockey Association, 18, 19, 20
World Junior Championships, 1978, 9, 66, 67, 69

Ziegler, John, Jr., 50